Canoeing Down Everest

Canoeing Down Everest

by

Mike Jones

HODDER AND STOUGHTON

LONDON SYDNEY AUCKLAND TORONTO

For Mum

British Library Cataloguing in Publication Data
Jones, Mike
    Canoeing down Everest.
    1. Canoes and canoeing – Everest, Mount
    I. Title
    797.1'22'095496   GV776.81.N/

    ISBN 0 340 22847 4

Mike Jones

MIKE JONES WAS the sort of person who never just got his feet wet in a project. Typically, he would jump into it right up to his neck, whether or not he knew exactly what he was doing. His overwhelming confidence in what he did or planned would first of all convince everyone he spoke to that he was completely mad. Then, when you realised he was serious, you either had to move away to avoid getting involved, or, far more likely and more often, you became so enthusiastic that you would find yourself bending over backwards to help him in any way possible.

The enthusiasm with which he undertook anything he did affected everyone around. Once an expedition had been decided upon he would devote his full energies and attention to the job in hand until it had been completed, and similarly he would expect equal effort from the rest of us.

His ideas were endless, some more feasible than others. During our discussions for future expeditions the possible ideas would be met by nods all round, the impossible would immediately strike everyone silent, until finally we all realised that the scheme in question was 'a little over the top' and relieved laughter would break out, bringing relief all round. The number of ideas were matched only by their scale and imagination. Recent additions to the list for the future ranged from parachuting canoes into the jungle to the Niagara Falls.

Mike's plans usually had one great flaw in them – time. He was never able to fit them into a twenty-four hour day, and all his calculations contained the mystical belief that all the traffic lights en route would be at green. This always set impossible targets on our trips and no matter how logically we could point out to Mike that he had drastically under-estimated the time factor, he would characteristically brush away all objections. This led to his famous estimate of 'twelve days to Kathmandu', and to one situation when Roger and Mike found themselves in the wrong country, on the wrong side of the Channel and 150 miles away from where they had arranged to pick up three people in a bus shelter.

A question which occurred to many people, was finally put to Mike by a young boy at the end of a lecture in Australia, when, in front of the audience he asked, 'Dr Jones, when are you going to grow up?' Mike answered in his own way by going out next day and spending twenty dollars to have a T-shirt printed with 'I've grown up' written proudly across the front.

The concept of danger never really worried him, and when it came to near misses, Mike was in a class of his own. During an expedition down the Blue Nile a crocodile suddenly appeared in the water between Mick Hopkinson and Mike's boat. Instinctively, Hoppy snatched for his revolver and, squinting to take aim, he found to his horror that the sights were crowded not only with the crocodile, but also by the disorganised figure of Mike struggling desperately with his movie camera and shouting to Hoppy to hold his fire until he had focused. Fortunately the crocodile was camera shy and submerged before any real harm was done.

Tragically Mike was killed this summer on the Braldu River in Pakistan attempting to save the life of his friend. His death came as a great shock to everyone who knew him. In canoeing circles Mike was a forward and dynamic figure. He had led expeditions to Austria, Africa, South America and Asia. Throughout the world he had made many friends, from Dudley Road Hospital where he did his medical training to Australia where he worked as a radio doctor. Most of all Mike will be missed for his warmth, friendship and relentless enthusiasm for life which continually kept him on the move and which infected everyone around him.

ROGER HUYTON
MICK HOPKINSON
September 1978

Contents

Illustrations

ACKNOWLEDGMENTS

Photographs by Leo Dickinson, cartoon on p. 15 by Don Charlesworth.

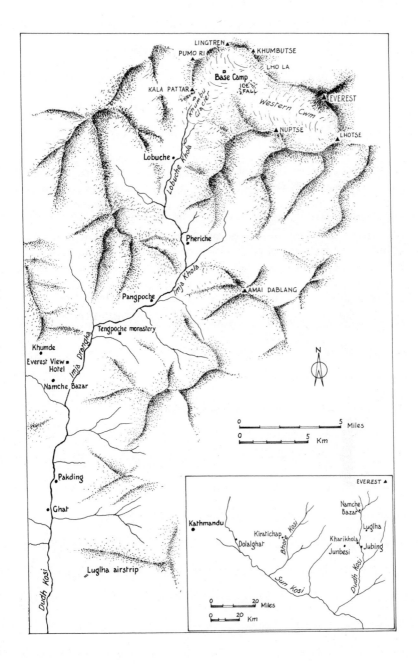

MIKE JONES WAS the instigator and inspiration of a small group of Britons who led the world in expedition canoeing. In his short life the succession of feats he achieved on white water were more than the equivalent of an ascent of Everest. He also possessed a very real courage which, apart from earning him recognition as the world's premier expedition canoeist, eventually and tragically cost him his life, when he went to the help of a friend in trouble.

CHRIS BONINGTON

1

What goes up . . .

DISCOVERED IN 1849, NAMED after George Everest in 1853, flown over in the 1930s, climbed in 1953, a woman has stood on the top, the Japanese have skied down it and in 1975 Haston and Scott scaled it the hard way up the south-west face and became the first Britons to stand on its summit. In 1976 I decided that I would canoe down it. 'It' is Mount Everest, at 29,028 feet the highest mountain in the world.

Situated in the Himalayan chain forming a great dividing range between Nepal and Tibet it has, since it was discovered, exerted a magnetic attraction on climbers and mountaineers. Much money has been spent, energy expended and many lives have been lost trying to attain the few square feet of snow where Hillary and Tenzing first stood in 1953 and so became the first men to reach the 'rooftop of the world', the point at which man can go no higher.

There are many glaciers moving slowly downhill in the Everest area and some of their surfaces are pock-marked by lakes filled with melt water. These lakes are indentations in the glaciers' surfaces and vary considerably in size but one of the larger ones is at about 17,500 feet, near the foot of the Khumbu Glacier. From this lake streams of water – first the Imja Khola, then the Imja Dranka – trickle their way through a terminal moraine formed of ice débris, rubble and stones until a few thousand feet further down, the water comes together to form the start of the Dudh Kosi River, a racing mountain torrent, a thundering mass of white water, a veritable liquid Cresta Run. For eighty miles it foams, plummets and churns its way through a series of wild and breathtaking gorges until, thirteen thousand feet below, its

11

power spent, it empties itself into the Sun Kosi River, from there into the Arun and from thence into the Ganges.

From information I had obtained talking to mountaineers and from looking at their photographs, I thought that it might well be possible for me to canoe round the lake, although it was sometimes frozen over and at other times jam-packed with blocks of ice, make a quick portage through the moraine and then come hurtling down the highest, fastest, steepest river in the world.

I would use a frail, thirteen foot fibre-glass kayak, to fall out of which would be to court disaster for there would be little chance of swimming in such icy, turbulent water. Barely above freezing point, travelling in places at more than thirty miles an hour over a rough bed strewn with boulders, such a river would offer a great challenge; it would surely be the most exhilarating white water canoeing that existed. At that height above sea level the air would be so thinned of oxygen that I would scarcely be able to breathe, which would sap my strength and so make it difficult to exert muscle power on my paddles for any length of time. Unlike a mountaineer I would not be able to stop and rest whenever I felt like it, but would be forced into long bursts of explosive action as I whirled down the river. The challenge was irresistible.

It would be necessary to take others with me, some canoeists, a back-up group to help from the bank and perhaps some photographers, for a film might defray the cost of mounting such an expedition. Without a back-up team we would have to carry all our food, clothing, tents and sleeping bags with us in the canoes. Although I had done such a trip, I knew that the gear made the canoes heavy, unwieldy and too difficult to manage in very rough water. It would be safer to have porters carry all the impedimenta when dealing with a Himalayan river. The back-up team would be able to rescue us if we got into difficulties on the water, they could run the camp sites and organise our porters. Porters would be needed not only to hump all our gear but to carry spare canoes, for if everything I had heard was true, we would need at least two craft each as the rocky river bed was sure to inflict considerable damage.

The more I thought about the expedition, the larger it became. As it grew in complexity in my mind and as the details proliferated, I realised that I still did not have the answer to the most important question of all: would there be enough water in the Dudh Kosi for our boats? At what time of year and how much? A canoeist's nightmare is to drag his craft all the way up to some inaccessible spot only to find that there is insufficient water in the river to enable his canoe to float. Would the Dudh Kosi have enough melt water from Everest before the monsoons arrived to let us clear the rough river bed, or would we have to walk up there during the monsoons to ensure that we arrived at the top at the time of maximum flood? We would have to time the whole expedition most carefully.

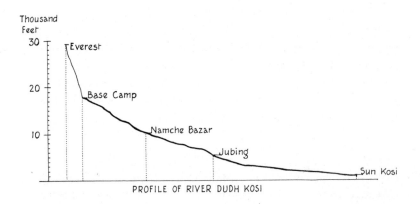

PROFILE OF RIVER DUDH KOSI

The aim of the expedition would be to achieve the world record for altitude canoeing, first by paddling along the lake at 17,500 feet and then by coming down from the top of the highest river in the world. The altitude record in 1975 was held by the West Germans who had canoed on the Indus River at about 12,000 feet but I would be starting 5,500 feet higher and descending to 4,000 feet in under eighty miles.

England can offer few difficult complex stretches of water

on which to canoe. Just occasionally, after heavy rain, there are one or two places which, when in full flood, cause one to look at them first, study them, look again and then go down them in trepidation, but there is nothing in the whole of the British Isles to compare with the Alpine streams, let alone the Himalayas. The Dudh Kosi would be a tremendous challenge for the whole of its entire length.

To give some idea of the steepness of the gradient it would offer, the Colorado River, running through the Grand Canyon, falls at ten feet per mile and the specially-built artificial gradient at Augsburg, where the Olympic canoe slalom course was held in 1972 and where championships are now decided, has been made to fall at fifty feet per mile, but the Dudh Kosi falls at 280 feet per mile, which is more than five times as much as the Olympic slalom course. Certainly no one before would ever have canoed down such a gradient.

Dudh Kosi translated from the Nepalese means 'river of milk' for not only does it have a very milky colour because of all the silt it carries from the moraine, but its bed is strewn with jagged rocky boulders which churn the already racing water into a seething creamy whiteness. Never smooth nor still, there were said to be few calm patches on the upper reaches of the Dudh Kosi.

Canoe down Everest? People were incredulous when I told them of my plans. Some people thought that we were going to crampon our way to the icy top and then toboggan down, with or without parachutes, sitting on our canoes in much the same way as the Japanese had ski-parachuted down. But surely it's all frozen ice up there? Is there really a river? The most favourable reaction seemed to vary charitably from considering us slightly mad to the more common 'bloody crazy'. Even the canoeing press billed it as a suicide trip, although they appeared to be considerably relieved when they found out that there actually was a river which flowed down from Everest.

Even the well-known literary agent who had represented many famous mountaineers and adventurers such as Chris Bonington and Wally Herbert thought the trip so wild, hare-brained and dangerous that when I approached him to

14

represent me, he politely turned me down. Even I was taken aback by his morbid predictions. He had been to Nepal and had walked along the banks of the Dudh Kosi during the post-monsoon period when it was low, and even then the turbulent river had been swirling and foaming. I would have to go when the river was in full spate to take advantage of the greater amount of water in the bed, which would help me to go over most of the rocks. He wrote to me saying:

I must have walked at least ten miles within a few yards of the Dudh Kosi and could get a good view of it from the mountain trails for at least another ten or twenty miles. Even in October it was 'white water' almost the whole way and because it is glacier-fed the water in the river is extremely cold. In view of this first-hand experience, I am afraid that I do not feel inclined to be associated with such a hazardous enterprise where the risk of losing at least one or two of the canoe team would be very high. So with great regret I think you had better count me out.

And yet I was optimistic. Over the space of six years, I had been involved with and led expeditions which had notched up many firsts on some of the world's most notorious rivers. Invariably we had proved the pundits wrong who gave us no more than an outside chance and we had been successful. I had canoed in Europe and the Alps, in Africa, in South America, in New Zealand and in the United States and all had gone well. This trip looked like being no different.

I rang Chris Bonington and asked him his opinion. 'Yes, I think it will go. Although it does look bloody difficult. It must rank in canoeing terms the same as climbing Everest – the dangers are about the same.'

Had I known at the time that the chances of being killed when climbing Everest are one in seven, then perhaps I would have thought differently!

Nowadays Bonington is a household name, his books sell by the thousand, his lectures are packed out and his mountaineering epics, recorded in celluloid on Everest and Annapurna, have made him world famous. But when I first met him he was working for the *Daily Telegraph* Magazine and I was only seventeen.

It was in 1969 and he had been sent out by his magazine to cover an eighty-mile descent by canoe of the Swiss river Inn which I was about to make. It was the first ever descent of this part of the river and was described by Bonington in the subsequent feature in the magazine as 'equivalent to the North Face of the Eiger'. I was most impressed by his frankness, openness and friendly nature. Over the years I have often consulted Chris and he has always given me much helpful advice on the various projects with which I have been involved.

Now he suggested that I ring Dr Peter Steele for a second opinion, as he was both a very experienced climber, a mountaineer and also a keen canoeist. He had moreover lived for some time in Nepal. An accomplished author, he has written several books on his climbing exploits and on Himalayan travel.

Always on the move, I was lucky to catch him. He was in the throes of packing his belongings into trunks and with his family emigrating to practise medicine in Canada. He gave me his opinion:

'Mike, it really is difficult canoeing and in monsoon it is colossal. And it's a hell of a walk to get there. Why not go for the Sun Kosi; at least you have a road nearby.'

I charted the course of the Sun Kosi on a map. The Sun Kosi is the river which the Dudh Kosi empties into before heading eastwards to join the Arun and the Ganges. It started at a mere four thousand feet, it looked wide and meandering; it would not offer the same sport and excitement as the racing, turbulent Dudh Kosi.

Perhaps I ought to go down to Bristol however to discuss things with Peter Steele. He had some slides of the river which would be a great help. But he altered his plans and left for Canada before I could get there.

Filled with indecision and misgiving, unsure and undecided, I wavered between the lure of the Dudh Kosi and the easier Sun Kosi. Then I made up my mind. The attraction of Everest was irresistible. I would get up to the Base Camp and from there to the foot of the Khumbu

Glacier. I would attempt the world record altitude for canoeing and endeavour to come down the highest river in the world. I would not settle for second best.

If Everest in the form of the turbulent Dudh Kosi was canoeable, I was going to do it.

2

Planning

EXPEDITIONS COME IN MANY shapes and sizes. They vary from the small and compact team made up of a few individuals who finance themselves and without a tremendous fanfare of publicity set off to do their own thing, to the massive modern day Himalayan expeditions with many sponsors and a huge publicity machine keeping the public informed through the press and TV of every move the expedition makes. Our expedition was to fall nicely between the two.

Himalayan expeditions nowadays are a complicated business. They invariably involve having to wade through a mass of paperwork, red tape and bureaucracy before getting under way and need an energetic businesslike approach if one is to attract sponsorship. This is the only way one can justify and embark upon these expensive projects.

My Everest trip would have to be a bit of a one-man show with myself at the helm. I would need to combine the roles and skills of fundraiser, publicity organiser, coordinator of equipment and PR man in addition to working 120 hours a week as a houseman in a busy peripheral Birmingham hospital – and competing on a regular basis at nationwide slalom and white water events.

I was extremely fortunate in working for two tremendous 'chiefs' – medical jargon for consultant. Allan Clain, surgeon, and Brian McConkey, physician at Dudley Road Hospital bore the brunt of my dual roles of working for the NHS as well as flat out organising our Everest trip. They became used to me disappearing in the middle of ward rounds to answer innumerable phone calls, fleeing outpatient clinics to attend meetings and give interviews, and racing off to go

19

training on local streams and rivers. They took it with wondrous good humour.

Medical secretary Lynn Smith worked like a slave in her own time on my letters and mass of correspondence. Nothing was too much trouble or took too much time, from a letter requesting tea-bags to one requesting £10,000. Perhaps it made a welcome change from typing routine medical discharge letters.

Having decided on an objective, my first priority was to select a team. I resolved from the start to assemble a collection of paddlers I knew well. From bitter experience I had found that the ultimate success and enjoyment of any expedition depends to a greater extent upon the participants. A team selected upon the basis of merit, rather than friendship and intimate knowledge of each other's strengths and weaknesses, never has that final degree of cohesion and drive that is required to succeed.

My own qualifications and experience for leading a major canoe expedition had been built up over the years.

It had all started off on a wintry Sunday morning in 1965 when, aged fourteen, I persuaded my elder sister Christine to part with her much-prized canvas folding kayak, and, with father at the wheel of an old battered 100E Ford Popular and the canoe perched precariously on the roof, we headed up into the Yorkshire Dales to take on the icy waters of the River Wharfe. It was an exhilarating and exciting day, with the river running high and offering some superb sport. I was well and truly bitten by the canoeing bug by the end of the day, despite the fact that I spent more time capsizing and swimming than canoeing.

That much wiser for the experience, I resolved that night to learn the eskimo roll, which is the name given to the way a canoeist rights his upturned craft without abandoning it. Upside down under water, he pushes on the paddle, using it as a lever to fetch the craft the right way up.

The following week I joined the school canoe club run by Geoff Smith, an affable chemistry master, and spent the next few weeks perfecting the art of eskimo rolling in the humid chlorine-filled atmosphere of the Oakbank Grammar School swimming pool. By the end I could turn over and over, to right or left, with my head going through 360° without gasping for breath or swallowing the pool.

In spring we were ready to tackle more of the rapids of the Wharfe, Ure, Swale, Nidd and Lune, all of which are encompassed within a forty-mile radius of Keighley. We spent many an exciting and action-packed weekend exploring and shooting rapids such as Hack Falls on the Ure and Gastrill Strid and the Strid on the Wharfe. The latter has claimed many lives, since at this point the river is badly undercut and has worn away a series of underwater caves from which there is little likelihood of a swimmer escaping.

From Yorkshire I progressed to rivers further afield. The Welsh Dee has for many years been one of the best rough water rivers in the UK. From the Chain Bridge Hotel, where the river narrows to twenty feet or so to form an S-shaped rapid, appropriately named the Serpent's Tail, to Llangollen Town are a series of rapids and falls which in low water are little more than rock-littered chutes. In winter conditions they are racing torrents, eager to capsize the unwary in the icy water and smash the canoes on to the rocks.

In those early days I took up slalom canoeing, which consists of racing against the clock between poles hung over the rapids, and this branch of the sport soon became my main recreational activity. It took me two years to reach division one, the top division of slalom competition, and I had to spend many hours travelling long distances to reach the major events. In March, we would brave the invariably wet and windy weather to camp on a mud-locked camp site on the banks of the Lune at Sedbergh. Easter and August Bank Holiday saw convoys of canoeists heading north to compete at Grandtully on the banks of the Tay, forty miles north of Perth. The river at this point falls steeply through a labyrinth of boulder chokes, and large rocks litter the course of the river bed. In high water it is probably the best slalom course in the British Isles, testing even the most experienced.

In September we would travel to the Serpent's Tail Slalom and three weeks later hordes of canoeists would once again descend on the sleepy town of Llangollen to compete on the rapids running beneath the Town Bridge, offering spectacular spectator sport for any tourists passing through on their way to North Wales.

In 1969 Jeff Slater, a nineteen-year-old Yorkshire student who was waiting to go up to Cambridge University, decided to put an expedition together to canoe on the River Inn and he asked me if I would like to go along with him. I was seventeen at the time and jumped at the chance, working feverishly at a variety of jobs in the holidays for five weeks in order to raise my own individual contribution to the expedition's funds. Jeff planned to take five other paddlers out to Switzerland with him and to shoot eighty miles of the Inn, large sections of which were rated by continental canoeists as impossible. For two months Jeff worked at putting his plans together; he managed to obtain the sponsorship of the *Daily Telegraph* magazine and to persuade Volkswagen to loan him a microbus.

By mid-July we were bucketing along in the sponsored Volkswagen for three weeks' training in Germany and Austria. What was intended as a warm-up was a baptism of fire. All the paddlers were much more experienced than I was and we hit the rivers in high flood. In spate, it was desperate stuff and never before had I seen rivers falling so precipitously and with so many water and rock hazards. A missed break-out a few feet off line and you were in serious difficulties.

We arrived at St Moritz after our warm-up and, driving up alongside the Inn gorge from the Austrian border, we realised why the Inn had earned itself the reputation of the hardest stretch of water in Europe. Confined within a steep-sided gorge, even from 1,000 feet up, the rapids looked colossal. The descent took five days and it was without doubt the hardest piece of water anyone in the team had tackled and in those five days we lost eight canoes and Trevor Eastwood, a Bradford engineer, almost lost his life. Chasing us down the bank and abseiling into the gorge to film and photograph our progress was Chris Bonington, then working as a freelance photojournalist.

It was at times extremely frightening and yet very exciting and an absorbing introduction to big water canoeing, where the stakes are so high. My appetite for adventure was whetted but it was almost two years before I was off again, this time to shoot 200 miles of the Colorado River running through the Grand Canyon in the USA – a descent of incredible beauty with some fierce, wild and untamed rapids.

By now I was an undergraduate studying medicine at Birmingham University. I would finish lectures on Friday evenings, occasionally even missing them altogether, and race off to canoe events all over the country, for the dedicated grind of medical study in the lecture theatre did not inspire me in the way that countrywide canoeing competitions did. As for the social life at Birmingham, that was hectic. It demanded stamina, strong nerves and a stout constitution.

In the autumn term of 1971, instead of devoting my full attentions to 'Herbert' our dissection corpse and becoming acquainted with the finer points of human anatomy, I began planning a descent by canoe of the African Blue Nile in Ethiopia. For full measure I had also been appointed team manager of a British Universities Slalom and White Water Team competing in three international slalom events in Austria, Switzerland and Czechoslovakia in late June and July of 1972. It looked like being a busy summer.

Throughout the winter and spring of 1971–72 I planned the two trips and in June, within a few hours of completing 2nd MB exams, an important milestone in any medical student's career, and without waiting for the results, I left for Austria. Once again the rivers were running high, swollen with melt waters from the previous winter's heavy snowfall. We competed with considerable success in slaloms at Muota in Switzerland, Spittal in Austria and in early July at Lipno in Czechoslovakia.

Three weeks later, with reactions speeded up and that much fitter, we arrived back in England and set about finalising plans for the Nile journey. I had succeeded in obtaining financial backing from the Winston Churchill Trust for this expedition which was going to be carried out with five people, Mick Hopkinson and I doing most of the canoeing. We would carry food and sleeping bags with us in our canoes and camp out at night beside the river. Chris Bonington however had warned me that two people on previous expeditions had been killed by bandits and that he himself had been ambushed in 1968, so he advised me to take some guns so that we could defend ourselves in case of trouble. In a whirlwind of activity our plans were put into action and within a week of arriving home I was on a flight out to Africa.

The expedition's start would have made a fine episode for the 'Goodies'. I arrived at Heathrow, my canoe on my shoulder, and much to everyone's amazement tried booking it on to the plane as hand baggage and eventually succeeded in getting it aboard as such, saving myself several thousand pounds.

I had left several days before everyone else and managed to get arrested in Cairo Airport for illegal possession of two .45 calibre revolvers and a double-barrelled shotgun with sawn off barrels which I was carrying around the airport foyer. Of course I should have known better since the Arab-Israeli problem was at its height and even in normal times my Che Guevara appearance would have raised a few eyebrows. In those troubled times I survived barely a minute before being pounced upon by armed guards and locked up. Eventually I was released and headed out to Ethiopia.

The Blue Nile runs from Lake Tana, its source, for 500 miles through Ethiopia until it empties into the Sudan and joins up with the White Nile at Khartoum. There have been numerous attempts to navigate the Blue Nile, most of which have begun from Shafartak Bridge which carries the road across the river 220 miles downstream from its source, since the rapids from here down to the Sudan are much less severe than those in the upper section. As early as 1903, Bill McMillan, an American big game hunter, tried to descend the Blue Nile, but his specially-constructed steel boats were wrecked after only five miles. As they walked back to Addis Ababa, one of his team was unfortunate enough to have his testicles cut off by a native. A later expedition by Herbert and Mary Rittlinger had to give up when her canoe was bitten in half by a crocodile. In 1962 Dr Amoudruz from the Canoe Club of Geneva fared even worse for he was attacked by Shifta, as the local bandits are called, and two of his party of six were killed. Three years later, Arne Rubin from Sweden attempted a solo descent. Attacked numerous times by crocodiles, he beat them off with empty Coca-Cola bottles, but eventually he capsized and lost all his equipment. John Blashford Snell's 1968 English expedition in the same area lost a man by drowning.

It was against this background that Mick Hopkinson and I spent two weeks alone on the Blue Nile: one of the most hair-raising experiences of my life. Maps of the area were non-existent and we navigated with the aid of a cutting out of the *Daily Telegraph* Magazine sellotaped on to the front deck of my canoe. Within thirty miles of our start we hit the Tissisat Falls, the second largest in Africa. Over 180 feet high, the thundering mass of white water drops over a sheet basalt ledge into a seething pool. We spent several tense hours ferry gliding from one island to the next at the top of the falls, trying not to be swept over the edge as we struggled to find the river bank to portage round them.

Below the falls the river drops into a formidable thirty-mile gorge of grade six canoeing – that is the hardest grade of all with ultimate risk to life. It was desperate stuff with no bank support party and no back-up facilities to assist us if we got into difficulties. It took us three days to shoot through the gorge and just as we were getting on to smaller rapids and hoping for an easier time, we were ambushed and shot up by bandits.

I spent my twenty-first birthday huddled in a soaking wet sleeping bag with a loaded .45 revolver in my hand. I woke at dawn to find the gun fully cocked, my finger curled round the trigger and the gun pointing at Mick Hopkinson's head. The traditional birthday went out of the window and I celebrated with a piece of Kendal mint cake and an oatmeal block.

But that was a feast for us as we had rapidly exhausted our food supplies and for three days we had to eat potatoes bought from some friendly natives. We then entered a section where, for 150 miles, we were repeatedly attacked by giant, twenty-foot crocodiles. Three thousand miles away, in Munich, people were watching the Olympic canoe sprint championships, not realising that another kind of world record was being broken in Ethiopia. A gold medal is supposed to be an athlete's ultimate motivation but few people have even been chased by a six-metre crocodile whilst in a canoe . . . Mick Hopkinson, who is short-sighted, was more of a danger to me than the crocodiles as he blasted away with a shotgun, but we managed to paddle out of trouble and succeed with our expedition: after twelve days on the river we were immensely relieved to escape with our lives.

It seemed an obvious choice for my partner on the Blue Nile, Mick Hopkinson, to be my deputy leader on the new Dudh Kosi expedition. Despite the fact that Mick lives only a few miles from my home in Keighley, our paths rarely crossed and it was not until he came to Ethiopia with me in 1972 that I really got to know him. Mick is a geography master at Bradford's Cardinal Hinsley School and they had given him paid leave of absence to go to Africa. Several years older than myself, he has a somewhat calming influence on my more hare-brained ideas. He is extremely strong, a superb technician on water and, despite the fact that he has to wear glasses which invariably mist up or become dislodged or fall off in rough water, he has an excellent eye for a line down rapids. We had worked well together on the Nile, especially in the difficult gorge section below Tissisat, and we had subsequently built up a fine working partnership on trips to Austria, Germany and Switzerland. At one point we had become serious C2 white water racers and had even managed to achieve respectable results in the British Championships. (A C2 class boat is a Canadian canoe paddled by two people kneeling, each wielding a single blade.) When I approached him to ask if he would like to come to Nepal, he seemed delighted and thought that he might be able to persuade his school to give him three months' unpaid leave of absence.

John Liddell, a longstanding friend from Grand Canyon days, had been involved with our plans from the beginning and was an obvious choice for inclusion. His father is a solicitor in Solihull, the stockbroker belt of Birmingham, and John went to public school but despite this handicap is still very down to earth. He has a penchant for Mini cars, which he drives like Jackie Stewart, and will happily point out on the drive from the town to the large detached house in the country where he lives with his parents, the various sites of numerous crashes in which in some mysterious way, a malevolent fate has somehow, quite inexplicably, managed to involve John and his beloved Minis. John's Minis, 'truth to tell', were always being brilliantly driven at the time and must have been attacked by a corner that moved or an aggressive lamp-post that rushed out into the street without due regard to other people's safety.

John is very much an 'on' or 'off' canoeist. He might be seen canoeing every weekend for three months and not be seen again for another year. John's lighthearted and humorous manner masks the activities of a character of determination and steely courage. He eagerly accepted my invitation and resigned his job as an accountant to come on the trip.

I had decided to take a team of six canoeists with me to Nepal. Six is ideal, since we could then work in two groups of three which is a safe number to work independently of each other whilst on the river, yet sufficient for help should anything go wrong. I now had Mick Hopkinson, John Liddell and myself, so had to start looking around for another three members. There were no end of volunteers and everyone started making suggestions of other possible canoeists.

Robert Hastings, a Leamington student, seemed a name which cropped up frequently. He is a warm, likeable person, very hard working and always willing to teach or give a helping hand. He is also very practical and is forever designing and building new gadgets. He is also a formidable canoeist, having been in the British team since the age of sixteen.

At that point in time Rob was working as a technician in the art department of Cardiff College of Art. Before inviting him to join the expedition, I asked him to come as a driver with a British Universities team I was taking out to Zwickau in East Germany. It was May 1975 and Rob was everything I expected and he was immediately taken with my plans. He was coming up to Birmingham in September to take a one-year Dip Ed course and would be able to help me with the vast amount of paperwork the expedition was going to involve.

I started asking around for a further two paddlers. Eventually after discussion with Mick Hopkinson I settled on Roger Huyton and Dave Manby.

It was typical of my lifestyle then that Roger was invited largely because he was able to survive the initiation test posed by a twenty-four-hour round trip to Paris to a party. Roger Huyton was studying at London University and was due to complete his degree in the summer of 1976. Although he had been in the British Junior Slalom team, he had lost interest in competitive canoeing and not done any serious paddling for over two years. Mick Hopkinson strongly recommended him and Rog, as he became known, with his incessant smile and total unselfishness was an invaluable member.

Dave Manby at twenty-one would be the youngest member of the team. His father ran a preparatory school near Shrewsbury and Dave was leading a rather chequered life at Nottingham University, whilst trying to study civil engineering. He had a colossal mop of long straggling hair, an unkempt beard and a pair of round NHS specs. He invariably wore pullovers with holes in the elbows and oily, torn jeans. This sloppy dress was intentional for Dave's hero was Doug Scott, the first Englishman to stand on top of Everest, and Dave wished to copy him sartorially. As Mick Hopkinson remarked, Dave's pullovers all had 'Moss Bros' labels inside, so they had come from one of the best outfitting concerns in the country, but Dave had deliberately gone on wearing them into holes in order to cultivate the way-out external appearance he liked. It only served to mask his real quality. He would be an asset to any expedition.

There were other paddlers whom I would have liked to have asked to come but many found it difficult to spare the time. Some had other commitments or were unable to get leave of absence for three months. For I had estimated that it would take us at least that length of time to drive out to

Kathmandu, walk up to Everest Base Camp, canoe down the Dudh Kosi and drive home again. It was, as someone remarked, almost four expeditions in one.

I now had the basis of a team on which I could build and my next important decision was to choose a date for our attempt. The monsoon in Nepal lasts from July until mid-September. From photographs I had seen of the Dudh Kosi and film taken by Chris Bonington on his walk up to Everest Base Camp, the ideal time appeared to be late August, when the river would be swollen with the monsoon rains. Although this makes the river level higher and produces more rapids, it lessens the chances of breaking canoes up on submerged rocks. That would mean walking up to Everest at the height of the monsoon. After throwing the idea around we eventually decided to aim to start canoeing by September 1st, which left us barely a year to get things organised.

Finance looked like being a big problem. I sat down one night and with what scanty information I had, began to calculate how much the trip was going to cost. There were so many improbables and imponderables; porters, insurance, transport, food and accommodation. Items which would be sponsored, those things we would have to buy. Eventually in the early hours of the morning I came up with the figure of £2,000. I leaned back in my chair and ignoring all my calculations and postulations, doubled the £2,000. Four thousand pounds was what we were going to need. That in the end the trip cost £11,500 gives some idea of how far out my initial calculations were!

The next few months were spent desperately searching for a sponsor. Eventually a great weight was removed from my mind when HTV Ltd Cardiff purchased the TV rights and the *Observer* Colour Magazine the story and picture rights.

Leo Dickinson, a Bristol-based freelance film producer, was asked to film the expedition. A climber of some reputation, he spends much of his time making climbing documentaries. He is small, squat and in his late twenties. Extremely determined and forceful, he has the legendary artist's mercurial temperament. He has tremendous creative talent and his films of climbing the North Face of the Eiger, the Matterhorn and sledging across the Patagonian ice-cap have won him international acclaim.

Leo was living at Garstang near Preston so Mick and I decided to drive up to see him. We hoped to persuade him that we were good canoeists and that the trip would be a worthwhile investment of his time and talent, but we quite forgot that of the two canoes on the roof of the car, one had the front eighteen inches missing and the other was broken in two.

Since much of the Dudh Kosi is in a gorge, Leo asked if he could take two climbers along as assistants. They would be able to climb down the gorge sides and photograph us as we came through and would also be considerable assets should we get into any difficulties on the river and need someone who could abseil down to help us out or let down ropes from the cliff top to haul us up. Leo thought that there might also be a chance that he could put ropes across the gorge in some places and so get some straight shots of us as we came through head on. All ways round, a head for heights would be very useful for everyone on the trip. Leo chose his regular climbing companion Eric Jones, and a newcomer to us all, Geoff Tabbner.

Eric Jones is in his late thirties and one of Britain's top solo alpinists. Quiet, introspective and unassuming, he is a self-contained individual who over the years has gone his own way in climbing circles and notched up impressive solo climbs in this country and the Alps without creating a tremendous ballyhoo about it. We all took to him. Eric had not only climbed the North Face of the Eiger with a team of climbers but he had also solved the North Face of the Matterhorn and the right-hand pillar of Brouillard by climbing alone with an ice-pick in either hand and crampons on his feet. He is like a fly and goes straight up the steepest side of any mountain with no ropes and nothing to hold him if he should slip. He had never climbed in the Himalayas before and was pleased to fulfil a vital support role for us, whilst testing himself out at high altitude.

Geoff was a different kettle of fish. A salesman of

audio-visual aids, he had already been on one expedition to the Himalayas to climb Dhaulogiri but they had lost one man and failed to make the summit. Confident and self-assured, he was a smooth talker and the expedition diplomat on the journey overland as, having driven out before, he knew the pitfalls and hazards. He decided to bring his wife Joyce along with him too.

In the latter stages of the expedition more people were added, until the final complement was thirteen.

HTV wanted to have two cameramen and eventually Mick Reynolds, who had worked for HTV for some time, was given the job. I had my doubts about his fitness since he had taken very little exercise for several years and was fast approaching middle age. All these doubts were unfounded, as he rapidly regained his fitness on the walk and eventually made it to Base Camp Everest, where he could be seen racing around with a battery of cameras as though on a routine filming assignment in the main streets of Cardiff or Llangollen.

Leo's girlfriend, Barbara Lloyd, also decided to come along for the fun of it all. Her Irish Equity card did not seem to be helping her to find much work as an actress, so she thought she would join our expedition. The alternative was spending the summer renovating the small country house she and Leo had just bought in Old Sodbury, where Leo had decided to settle since much of his work now centred around HTV, Cardiff. She is a magnificent cook and excellent company.

The final inclusion in the team was John Gosling. John was an old friend of mine from Birmingham who at the time was working as a catering manager in Peterborough. Jovial, tending to overweight, he seemed the ideal person to help organise the massive logistics operation which had now developed with the inclusion of a film crew. He came up to Birmingham the weekend after my decision and we went to a local pub for lunch. He was delighted with the idea and agreed to take on the job of organising catering and acting as Base Camp manager and 'trouble shooter' on the bank. He was to be worth his not inconsiderable weight in gold.

The organisation in this country seemed to be progressing satisfactorily. Overseas I had written to Mike Cheney who at that time was working in Kathmandu for Mountain Travel, a concern run by Colonel Jimmy Roberts, who retired from the army several years ago and was one of the first people to realise the tourist potential for trekking in Nepal.

Mike Cheney was a wizened man in his early forties who looked much older. He had gone to Nepal several years previously and fallen in love with the countryside and the people. He loved expeditioneering and whilst most of his income came from organising treks for tourists, he spent a disproportionate amount of time and money organising, participating in, and administering mountaineering expeditions. He took to the problems of a canoe expedition like a duck to water and it was only through Mike's persistence and patience in the months preceding our arrival that our trip had such a smooth passage through the formalities and red-tape of Kathmandu. The Nepalese authorities do not allow anyone to arrive and then just wander up the mountain track to the Everest area. The right to use the Base Camp must be booked well in advance and only one group of climbers is allowed there at a time. Porters must be laid on to carry all the gear and details of equipment must also be cleared with the Nepalese authorities.

Transport looked like being a major headache. Initially, we had planned to fly out but with the massive amount of equipment thirteen people would need; at least twelve canoes, all the camera gear plus enough food for three months, tents, baggage rolls, rucksacks, clothes and camping extras, together with the cost of thirteen passenger seats, this looked like being financial suicide. I decided it would be best if we drove overland across Europe to Kathmandu. It might be a long journey, subject to delays and hold-ups at border crossings, there were risks of break-down and the petrol would be expensive, but it would be more economical in the long run than flying. What we needed was a huge vehicle.

With great generosity, Bristol Street Motors, the largest Ford distributors in the Midlands, with their headquarters in Birmingham, offered to lend us a fifteen-seater Ford

The canoeists: left to right John Gosling, Roger Huyton, John Liddell, Mick Hopkinson, Mike Jones, Dave Manby, Rob Hastings.

Break-down point in central Turkey, and a 400-mile return to Ankara for repairs.

Flood water on the road to Lahore.

Mick Reynolds films, Dave Manby contemplates pots in Kathmandu.

Transit Minibus for the expedition. Both Transit and Bristol Street were tremendous. Brand new with a diesel engine, cloth seats and a stereo system, they fitted it up with a tachometer so that it complied with EEC regulations and designed and built a special aluminium roof loader for us, costing over £1,000, for carrying all our gear. With its enormous, spacious interior and the most expensive roof rack ever made, we felt that it could be rated as the Rolls-Royce of the expedition world.

The next important decisions that had to be made concerned our gear, especially the canoes. Would we take standard makes with us or would we have craft specially built for the Himalayas?

Rough water canoeing, paddling down rapid rivers, was developed in Alpine countries as a summer alternative to winter ski-ing. Brought to Great Britain in the 1920s, the first boats used were folding kayaks constructed out of a canvas 'skin' fitted over a wooden framework. But canoeing today is like climbing was forty or fifty years ago, still in its infancy; the craft have already come a long way but now their method of manufacture is changing very rapidly. In 1963 fibre-glass canoes appeared. These were constructed by making mould sections of the deck, hull and seat in glass reinforced plastic (GRP) and 'seaming' together the deck and the hull, and then adding the seat unit. At first the GRP was made from glass matt and polyester resin but later woven rovings, a glass cloth was used. Roy Stayley of Streamlyte dominated production in this country in the Sixties and he later pioneered the use of carbon fibre in thin strands to reinforce very lightweight craft.

At first the International Canoe Federation did not take kindly to rigid fibre-glass boats and made them race in a separate World Slalom Championship class from folding canvas canoes. But after the 1963 races, they changed the rules and created a single K1 class which allowed both kinds to vie against each other in slalom and white water racing. This gave great momentum to changes in design and construction.

In 1964 the first white water racer was developed, when it was realised that a canoe designed to be manoeuvrable in a slalom course had different needs to one whose aim was to go in a straight line, racing over three to four miles of rapids. Racers were built with V-shaped hulls to slice through the water and they were made lighter and lighter to encourage speed and responsiveness.

In 1970 the polyester fabric Diolen was used although twice as expensive as glass matt, and then in 1972 Kevlar was introduced which is an aramid fibre fabric, stronger and more resilient to impact although six times as expensive as Diolen.

Where do the canoe designs come from? Roy Stayley's original canoes were designed by Keith White and were appropriately called the KW range. Subsequent designs numbered up to KW 7. In the latter Sixties, Graham Goldsmith and his brother Bob set up Gaybo and began importing designs from Pavel Bone, Toni Prijon and Klaus Lettmann and making these boats in this country. Their boats, designed abroad, dominated the competition market until the early Seventies.

In 1967 the Hartung range of canoes was introduced. This was a low buoyancy range specifically aimed at the competition market, and low volume canoes became increasingly popular as paddlers discovered that it was very easy to save several seconds in a slalom race by using these low volume boats, which could be ducked underneath the slalom gates.

In 1972 there was something of a backward trend, for the specially constructed Augsburg Olympic slalom course was relatively heavy water, so the manufacturers went back to the high volume designs of the mid-Sixties, such designs as the Olymp 4 and the Prijon 'L' or 'S' design. After the Olympic Games the trend was for lower and lower volume, the most revolutionary being those of Graham Mackereth of Pyranha Canoes in Warrington, whose Vedel range gained in popularity. In 1975 his Vedel SS took seventh and eighth places in the World Championships, the first time a British designed canoe had achieved success in the World Championships since the mid-Sixties.

Lower volume means that the canoes' stern and bow can be submerged but big buoyancy means that they are designed to negotiate large rapids. For Everest we wanted a medium buoyancy type going, contrary to recent trends, back to the designs used in 1972.

I decided that the canoes I wanted made specially for Everest would be of polyester resin reinforced with Kevlar fabric and built for me by Graham Mackereth of Pyranha.

Graham decided to take one of his very successful slalom canoe hulls, modify it slightly to make it more buoyant and build a higher and more buoyant deck on to it. The canoe was very manoeuvrable even in the most turbulent water and it proved ideal for the conditions we met. Our only problems were when we bolted a sixteen-pound TV camera on the front of the canoe, when it became understandably nose heavy and difficult to handle.

I wanted a high volume boat weighing no more than thirty pounds and thirteen feet in length. It would need to ride well above the water, shed waves quickly and be exceptionally manoeuvrable. The hull would need to have extra reinforcement under the seat at bow and stern, and a longitudinal wood strengthener would have to run along the centre of the hull to take the pounding it seemed likely to get. The conditions were likely to be so rigorous that hull and deck would have to be seamed both inside and out to give extra strength.

Each canoe would need a fail-safe footrest bar inside, so that no one could get trapped underwater and be unable to get out. If, for some reason, the canoeist's feet are forced underneath and past the footrest bar and it is solidly bolted to the side of the canoe, it is impossible to get your feet back other than by sheer brute strength. There have been several fatal accidents when people have become trapped in upturned canoes by their feet. But the fail-safe footrest is hinged at one end and swings back if there is trouble. My own preference was for an aluminium bar fibre-glassed into position but, since different people would be using the canoes each day, this would be impracticable and we would have to have adjustable footrests which could be changed to suit varying leg lengths.

Extra buoyancy would be necessary to reduce damage when the canoes got swamped and to help with their retrieval from the river if they floated away. Each canoe would also need to have a rope loop at stern and bow for people swimming in the water to catch hold of and be rescued by, or to retrieve the canoe.

Graham was an ebullient, hard-headed businessman, who had given up accountancy to found his own very successful and thriving canoe-building business. One of the few British canoe builders to design his own canoes, he works tremendously hard and his factory is a hive of activity seven days a week. Only six of our twelve canoes were ready when we left England, but he built the rest at fantastic speed and personally raced out after us to catch us up en route and deliver them. We were in Austria at the time and delighted to see him.

Paddles came from a variety of sources. Alistair Wilson supplied Lendal fibre-glass shafted white water blades which are the ones I like, for they are exceptionally light, spooned and curved to feather well but offering minimum air resistance. Most of the others however preferred the heavier Prijon blades. Everyone used right-hand feather blades and 215 centimetres seemed to be the most popular length.

A paddle to a canoeist is like an ice-axe to a mountaineer, personal, vital and private. Each person looks after his own and keeps it by him. To my surprise only one was broken and one lost down-river during the whole three months, out of the twenty we took with us.

Other important equipment included plastic crash helmets with slits in them to let the water out. Light and comfortable, these were to save team members from serious head injury should they be dragged along the bottom of the river or have their heads bounced against rocks. We also took life jackets, Thermawear vests, cagoules and wetsuit trousers.

The last two months before departure went by in a whirlwind of activity. There were sponsorship and publicity deals to be tied up, equipment to be checked and packed for the overland trip, late orders to be chased up and forgotten items of equipment begged or bought. An incessant stream of vehicles with girlfriends at the wheel left my flat to pick up missing or late items, and it seemed as though we would never be ready.

A week before we were due to leave, the canoe team with a film crew from 'Midlands Today' descended on Leamington Spa, where we had discovered a small sluice gate which, when opened, gave twenty yards or so of broken water. We spent a hilarious time ferrying cameramen and reporters stripped to their underpants across to a small island, from where they filmed and interviewed us as we cavorted in front of the cameras.

Catering was a major worry. John Gosling was working eighteen hours a day trying to get things ready in time so that we could leave as programmed. Over 200 letters had been written to foodstuff manufacturers and companies and many had responded magnificently, but there were the inevitable shortfalls and deficiencies. Rarely we had excesses, particularly of mackerel, of which we had enough to do justice to the catch from a large trawler and to this day John's cat is still eating the excess.

Those items in which we were deficient were purchased in a mammoth shopping spree from a local supermarket.

With one day to go the entire operation was moved to Rob Hastings' father's school hall in Leamington Spa. All the food had to be packed into sixty-pound food boxes which was the maximum weight the porters would carry. A production line of friends and relations was set up weighing out and labelling sugar, coffee, pancake mix and a thousand and one things which made up each food box. The boxes themselves had only been obtained the previous day and Tri-Wall Containers who supplied them had gone to great lengths to ensure they reached us on time.

Into each box we put enough food to last eighteen men for ten days and, when completed, each box was secured with waterproof tape and sealed inside heavy-duty thick gauge plastic fertiliser bags.

We worked into the early hours of the morning. Lists were typed, boxes stacked and labelled, equipment checked off and tested, inventories scrutinised for missing items and finally everything packed into the van. There was no way everything was going to be ready on time, so whilst the team made final preparations and sorted out last-minute details, I drove a hundred miles down to Cardiff to do a TV interview for HTV and meet Aled Vaughan, the Managing Director of Harlech.

I made it back to Birmingham late in the afternoon and worked through the evening and into the early hours of the morning packing up my room, answering urgent last-minute correspondence and making up a medical kit.

The next morning the whole team ate breakfast at Dudley Road Hospital. A telegram had arrived and I slit it open, smearing butter on the cut edges. It was from Vladivar Vodka, one of our last-minute sponsors, who had come in only three weeks previously by paying for the canoes. It read: 'Have a Vladimarvellous Time.' We certainly intended doing so!

3

Training in Europe

Goodbye Birmingham! Hello Frankfurt-on-Main!

This was to be the first stage of our journey to Everest.

Anyone who has learned to survive amongst the whirling traffic of Birmingham has a fair degree of character, competence and confidence. If he is wise however, he prays for benevolent providential guidance as he approaches the European roads, drivers and their idiosyncratic continental driving manners.

Frankfurt is probably the most important city in West Germany but, from our point of view, it was the focal point of the *Autobahn* system and would put us within striking distance of some of the finest and most exciting canoeing rivers in Europe. These were the rivers we needed, to work up into some sort of shape before setting off on the long trek to Everest. The journey was one which I had done many times before and after twenty-four hours of continuous driving, we arrived in Frankfurt. Here we were welcomed by an attractive young German teacher, Renate Kolloch, who was Mick Hopkinson's girlfriend and well known to us all. She had worked for some time in Bradford and spoke fluent English: she always seemed to be as at home in Yorkshire as she was in Germany.

It was dinner-time before we had finished off-loading equipment and food into the basement of the house which we were using as a temporary base. Work done, hot and sweaty on this equally hot day, we indulged ourselves by going for a swim in a large lagoon on the outskirts of the city. Then, in the world's sausage centre, what else but German garlic sausage, Swiss cheese, freshly baked hot crusty bread washed down with German beer. All this out in the open on a gloriously sunny day.

Our next destination was Augsburg, south of Munich,

where we were going to train on the Olympic slalom canoe course. We knew that the Dudh Kosi would be the most difficult white water any of us had ever been on, so we wanted to be in peak condition for it, fit, balanced and alert. There was nowhere in England with sufficiently difficult rapids and enough fast flowing water for us to experiment on, so we were going to tone up on Alpine streams. This practice was essential to help us learn to assess rough wild water and to enable us to read it at speed. The ability to do this is quickly lost without practice and it was vital that we should all be confident in our reactions under extreme conditions. The slalom course had been specially built for the 1972 Olympics and was a unique man-made rough water course of vast, smooth concrete rocks with an abundance of severe falls and rapids, all controlled by giant sluices. It was excellent training and we spent days sharpening up reflexes and toning up muscles, making the most of this magnificent facility.

Britain has done surprisingly well in world slalom races, considering that the sport is fairly new to this country and that we have few fast moving rivers. Britain had a world slalom champion in 1959 called Paul Farrant but tragically he was killed in a motorbike accident in 1960. From then on, canoeing in Britain seemed to explode, dominated by Dave Mitchell, who was British champion seven times between 1960 and 1970. In 1963 Dave won a bronze medal in the team event of the world championships and in 1967 he won a silver in the individual slalom, so we haven't fared too badly.

Whilst British canoeists have been improving, they have invented or borrowed various terms to describe the way rivers twist and flow, and have named the various techniques needed to manoeuvre canoes through falling breaking water. Before describing what happened to us on and in rivers, I would like to pause a moment to explain the terms I shall be using. There is a further glossary on page 191 for reference purposes.

The most essential technique is the eskimo roll, which I have already mentioned, for this rights the canoeist when he has been overturned by a wave.

40

When the water in a river meets a drop such as a weir, it falls smoothly over the ledge but at the bottom it performs a circular motion in an anti-clockwise direction, forming a stationary wave or *stopper* as it foams back on itself. The water nearest to the drop is sucked under and the top of this stationary wave is breaking and is technically known as an hydraulic jump. When a canoe hits the top of a stopper, the water pouring down the weir pushes on the back of the canoe and the water underneath it tries to suck it under. At the same time the front is resting on a breaking wave. The effect of all this water pushing on the back makes the front want to rear up vertically. To stop it doing this is difficult. It is essential that the paddler break through the wave quickly, either by travelling along it sideways to a break-out point or by shooting through it, or he may be tipped out. So when he hits the stopper he must press down hard on the wave with his paddle to stop being sucked in or up-ended. If the canoe is up-ended it is said to have performed *a loop*.

Where flowing water meets up against some hidden obstruction in the river bed such as a boulder, an unbroken stationary wave may exist on the surface which is called a *standing wave*. An exploding wave with a broken foaming top curling back on itself is called a *haystack*.

As a river races downstream it may meet water and rock hazards or *rapids*: a whole series of stepped rapids form a *cataract*. One large rapid with an appreciable drop over a short distance is called a *fall*. Where the moving water swirls into a vortex, it is called a *whirlpool*.

All the time the canoeist is paddling through hazards such as those named above, he is keeping his eye out for somewhere he can stop, pause, look ahead and plan his route. These areas of slack water usually lie behind obstructions in the river bed and are known as eddies or *break-outs*. If he sits in his canoe in a break-out and can see no way through ahead at all, the mass of jumbled boulders blocking his route is called a *rock choke*. He may then have to make his way back upstream, crossing the current by paddling the canoe at an acute angle which is called a *ferry glide*.

Moving water has been graded according to the severity of the rapids it contains. In this book I have used the following definitions: grade one for smooth moving water; grade two for moving water with occasional rocks; grade three for more rocks. Large falls but not continuous ones I have called grade four, but where there are long continuous unbroken stretches of rapids it is grade five. Grade six is the hardest there is and this type of water carries the ultimate risk to life for it is not possible to swim out of it.

We had finished our practice at Augsburg. Now I decided to move on to Lofer in Austria where I had competed as part of a British team in 1972 and 1974. In complete contrast to the Inn, the Saarlach River cuts a steep gorge at the edge of the town and produces a series of swift-flowing and specta-cular rapids.

In summer the local canoe club holds a canoe slalom above the town bridge, but they rarely venture below the bridge as there is a sign suspended from the wooden hand-rail which says 'Danger: Canoes Forbidden'. This is a great pity for the gorge provides over three miles of exhilarating canoeing: exciting stuff with stoppers, waterfalls, chutes and extremely testing water conditions.

I had arranged to shoot some film for 'News at Ten' and the gorge seemed an ideal place. We spent an afternoon performing as the cameras rolled, capsizing, righting ourselves, using stopper pressure waves to loop the canoe – that means, standing them on end – and thoroughly enjoying being on the water.

Next we headed for Spittal in Southern Austria. It is a famous town in the canoeing world and the World Championships were to be held there in 1977. When we arrived, the British team were trying to practise but there was so little water in the river that it was impossible to canoe. So next morning away we went to the River Izel and the Falls of Huben.

The Izel is barely sixty miles away but, despite setting out early, we did not reach the start at the foot of the Falls of Huben until eleven am. The tortuous road had wound its way alongside and although much higher than the river, we had caught odd glimpses of the fast, rock-studded rapids. At a much higher altitude and with a more reliable snow-melt the river was as I expected and would be a good test of fitness and skill.

All sports have their casualties and elements of danger. It is this total commitment to the contest between skill and danger that is the appeal in sports such as rock climbing and canoeing. Not that canoeing drowns many people a year in Britain. The figures* for the years between 1970 and 1976 are:

1970	16 deaths per year
1971	7 deaths per year
1972	16 deaths per year
1973	7 deaths per year
1974	11 deaths per year
1975	6 deaths per year
1976	8 deaths per year

When you think that most of these casualties were not experienced canoeists but individuals who went out unsupervised, you can see what a non-lethal sport it is. There are only about two or three deaths a year of experienced canoeists: one of these had met his end ten years before over the Falls of Huben. An English canoeist, he had mistakenly launched above instead of below the falls.

It was in 1965 that two Chalfont canoe club enthusiasts, Philip Sixsmith and Tim Ridehough, had come to the Izel. Apparently they had misunderstood instructions and, with the river running in very high flood, had launched above the falls and within a few hundred yards had rounded a corner only to encounter two enormous stoppers. Ridehough was caught in the first one, came out of his canoe and lost it downstream. He was swept to the bank and against a rock where he managed to crawl out of the river. Sixsmith made it through the stopper but was last seen alive by Ridehough as he was swept downstream. His body was recovered eight days later from the river over seventy miles further downstream.

At the time of this accident, approximately fifty miles

*Source: Oliver Cock, BCU.

away, the British slalom and white water team were competing at Spittal at the World Championships. A telephone message came through to the British team to say that Sixsmith had been lost in the river, so they abandoned the championships to go in search of him. As a result of this episode the slalom and white water committee passed a ruling that British canoeists must not paddle rivers in the immediate vicinity of an international competition where a British team was entered.

Conscious of Sixsmith's tragedy at this particular spot, we pushed our canoes into the River Izel with extreme caution. The entire team was on the water, including John Gosling and two English friends of his, Pete Henry and Tony Thompson.

Within a few seconds Gosling was in trouble, followed by Tony Thompson who was caught upside down against a rock and forced to abandon his canoe. Fast flowing, with few break-outs as the Izel was, Gosling was lucky to swim out on to the bank. Thompson was less fortunate and found himself swept on to and marooned on a rock in the centre of the river. Ropes were hurriedly sent for and, after taking a line across the river, Thompson was hauled to safety.

We continued down with no further major incidents and reached a point six miles on, where the river drops over three weirs. At one thirty pm I led down through the weirs and paddled to the left-hand bank where the Transit was waiting. The canoes were manhandled on to the trailer and we drove back to the start to repeat the descent. Our second shoot was not without incident either, and a third canoe was written off by Roger Huyton who failed to roll in the treacherous water and ended up having a long, cold swim.

In the gathering dusk we drove back, well satisfied with our immensely strenuous and exhausting efforts. At Spittal we found that our specially built 'Everest Elite' canoes had arrived from England so we loaded them up, ready to head through Innsbruck and across to Landeck, forty miles from the Swiss border, the following day.

Where the Rivers Sanna and Inn unite, is the sleepy Austrian town of Landeck. It is full of trinket and teashops for the tourists. Both rivers offer splendid canoeing and thirty miles away are the glacier-fed rapids of the Otz River which, late in the summer, swollen with melt water from the mountains, ranks as one of the best white water rivers in Austria.

Every year national slalom and white water races are held on the Sanna. Its small technical rapids are a canoeist's nightmare, looking notoriously easy to shoot, yet each year many canoes are written off.

Local canoeists ignore the more ferocious and larger rapids of the Inn, preferring to leave these to the more adventurous paddlers. From six miles above the town the river is a never ending series of water hazards, stoppers, breaking waves, and haystacks which require considerable skill and expertise in descending.

After two days on the Sanna and Inn, we travelled across to the Otz. We arrived too early in the day to catch the main melt water coming off the glacier. We lounged about in the café, drinking coffee and watching the rain come down.

At three pm we decided it was time to go on. The rain had ceased and the sun was shining weakly through a low bank of cloud. The river was now up and running high and fast. For over six miles it drops rapidly, producing sustained grade five paddling. Shallow, even in the centre no more than three or four feet deep, the speed is incredible. From the top to the bottom it is just like riding a roller coaster, with wave closely following wave in the centre of the river and at the edges many small notoriously deceptive stoppers.

Halfway down we met Hans Memminger. In his early thirties, he was a member of the German canoe team, until dropping out of competitive canoeing. He then took up a freelance career as a maker of canoe films in obscure corners of the world.

We pushed on together and reached the confluence of the Otz and Inn by four thirty pm. Riding a series of rapids with enormous rollers, which would have done justice to the Grand Canyon, we paddled downstream to our take out point.

Memminger had been in Nepal the previous year filming for TV. Adjourning to a café by the side of the river, he talked in broken English about his trip and we arranged to see his film on our way home.

We spent over a week at Landeck, in the morning repairing canoes and the afternoon dicing our way down the rapids of the Inn and Sanna.

At the end of the week, we headed up to Switzerland to tackle one of the most formidable sections of water in Europe, where the Inn crosses from Switzerland into Austria.

In 1969 when I was in Jeff Slater's team which canoed the Swiss Inn for the *Daily Telegraph* Magazine, we had missed out this particularly severe section of rapids known as the Finster Munster Shoot. This had already claimed several lives and it wasn't until 1973 that Mick Hopkinson and I made the first descent. I was still short of footage for 'News at Ten' and thought it would make spectacular film.

Customs formalities over, we crossed from Austria into Switzerland. From a thousand feet up we saw the river carving its way through the steep-sided gorge. The chute looked frightening. We drove three miles above the rapids and decided to launch the canoes where the road dropped down to meet the river at the entrance to the gorge section.

The canoes were unstrapped and unloaded. Whilst I filmed, everyone got ready and, scrambling down a scree slope, launched their canoes in the murky grey rushing water. I changed quickly, donning wetsuit trousers, a lightweight shirt and anorak, lifejacket, crash hat and neoprene spraysheet and lowered myself into my canoe, easing my 16mm camera waterproofed in a heavy duty plastic bag between my knees.

The three-mile lead-up took ten minutes and we practised break-outs and crossing the rapids as we went. The brink of the fall came into view; we found it completely altered from the previous year. Even the fifty-yard lead-up looked like one of the hardest pieces of water that I had seen with several enormous stoppers and standing waves leading into a giant, circling cauldron of water, some fifty feet in diameter. Looking downstream, there was only one exit to the right of a huge rock against which the river swirled and eddied. Even the exit looked treacherous, with a huge stopper guarding the top of the chute and a twenty-foot eighty-five degree wall of water racing down into a stopper and series of breaking waves. I hauled my canoe on to the bank and picked my way along the rocks to the top of the Finster Munster. It would make some spectacular filming and I set my camera up on the brink of the fall as Mick Hopkinson and John Liddell prepared for the chute.

John came through first. He took a bold line down the centre of the rapid, edged two big stoppers at the top and was thrown sideways by the final stopper before the chute. With a few well-timed back strokes he managed to reverse the canoe off the left-hand rock guarding the entrance to the chute and was swept over and down the chute broadside on, capsizing but rolling up effortlessly as he cleared the bottom stopper.

Mick Hopkinson did not fare quite so well. He capsized shortly after he hit the first stopper, failed on his first attempt to roll and barely succeeded on his second. I watched horrified as he was swept against the large rock which John had so narrowly missed and dropped the camera as he was wedged broadside on to the rock and swept underneath. It was exactly the same situation in which two Germans had drowned in 1968. I felt completely helpless as I raced along my rocky ledge up to a point directly opposite where Mick had disappeared. There was no sign of either Mick or the canoe as I desperately scanned the roaring waterfall. Roger Huyton, upstream of my position, began shouting and gesticulating madly and as I jerked around Mick re-appeared on the far side of the rock, still in his canoe, having survived being swept and trapped underneath the rock, his helmet twisted, and spray-sheet ripped half off. He was about to drop over an eight-foot vertical waterfall. Amazingly he managed to straighten the canoe and leaning back along the stern deck, he nose-dived into the splash pool beneath, capsized and rolled up looking somewhat the worse for wear.

I leapt into my canoe and paddled across to him. He was deathly white and visibly shaking. He held on to the side and tried to recover his breath and for several minutes was unable to say anything. Finally he gasped through clenched teeth, 'I hope you got it on film,' I knew I hadn't but hated to admit it and just nodded non-committally.

The next rapid, no more than one hundred yards downstream, is equally testing and for over half an hour we clambered and climbed over rocks by the side to decide on a line. At last we had it and with Mick bravely leading, we shot down in fine style without mishap. Exhausted, we drifted the remaining three miles to the finish, paddling across to beach our canoes on the bank. But the bank was in Austria; we had crossed the Swiss-Austrian border and were now without our passports. Up the road was a mile-long tailback of traffic and the van with all our dry clothes was out of sight. No amount of special pleading would persuade the customs officers to let us run up the waiting line of traffic, so we shivered for half an hour in the drizzle, miserably cold.

Much to my surprise we had got some excellent film out of the day's canoeing; it was shown on ITN's 'News at Ten' six days later.

On July 27th we started back towards Germany. There were boats to repair, the vehicle to be serviced and re-packed with the equipment and food we had left in Frankfurt, Tony Thompson and Pete Henry dropped off back in England and Geoff and Joyce Tabbner and Barbara Lloyd picked up for the overland journey, and a lot of details to sort out before we set off.

I decided to go back to England to tie up loose ends, whilst the rest of the team, with the exception of Roger, who was coming along to share the driving, waited in Frankfurt and sorted out the mass of gear we needed for the overland trip.

We drove through the night from Frankfurt arriving at Ostend to catch the five am ferry across the Channel. Leaving the Transit sitting on the quay, we walked aboard carrying canoes and baggage.

Landing at Dover, having snatched an hour's sleep on the boat, we spent an entertaining half hour fitting four canoes on to a double-decker bus to take them across to the customs area.

Then into a Hertz car and away to London, which we

Leo Dickinson organising his porter-loads of camera equipment.

The can of birthday beer being shared between twelve thirsty people.

Himalaya Hotel—floor space at thirty pence a night.

The taste of fibre-glass soon pervaded everything.　　　　　　So did the local leeches.

reached by eleven am. Roger disappeared in one direction whilst I raced off in another. There was film to be dropped off, newspaper reports filed, some late camera equipment picked up and a thousand and one minor things to be sorted out.

By six pm we had cleared up most of the loose ends and headed again towards Dover. Twenty miles south of London, speeding along at about seventy miles an hour, the front tyre blew out and the car careered madly off the road, ploughing into a grass bank. More delays, repairs and eventually we were on our way.

At last we reached Dover and leaving the car in the rental garage forecourt and with bulging rucksacks, raced to catch the nine pm ferry.

Immediately on landing we cleared customs and were relieved to see the Transit still standing on the waterfront. Roger drove, but barely more than ten miles outside Ostend the engine began spluttering and coughing. The fuel gauge showed empty and I cursed my own slackness for not checking the level before we left. Stopping and starting, we made another five or so miles as the last of the fuel made its way through the system, before grinding to a halt.

We were in the centre of a heavy industrial area and after searching unsuccessfully for fuel, we resigned ourselves to spending the night in the van.

At first light, I was woken by a tapping on the window. I rolled over in my sleeping bag, wiped the condensation from the window and looked out to see a jowl-faced character peering in. Roger was awake and clambered out of the door. Apparently the building we were next to was a railway shunting shed and we were parked across the railway line! I looked out and indeed we were. Roger explained our problem and the man disappeared off in the direction of the shed, only to reappear a few moments later with a great oily jug full of diesel fuel. Roger slid into the driving seat and a few minutes later, once the fuel had been pumped through, the engine fired and we were away. Ten minutes later we came to a petrol station which was open. The tank was quickly filled with diesel fuel before heading towards

Calais where Geoff and Joyce Tabbner and Barbara Lloyd were anxiously waiting.

Rapidly we loaded their gear into the back of the Transit and drove down through Belgium and on to the German *Autobahn*. It was a scorching hot day and the sun was beating down as we chugged along at fifty miles per hour. Finally, we arrived at Frankfurt late in the afternoon. The van was then loaded with equipment and food for the overland journey before, thankfully, I collapsed into my sleeping bag and slept undisturbed until late the following morning.

4

The Road to Kathmandu

THE ROAD TO KATHMANDU witnesses an increasing number of travellers each year. Twenty years ago travelling the 7,500 miles was a major undertaking with long stretches of pot-holed, dirt-track road, in dry weather providing swirling clouds of choking sand and dust, and in the wet, conditions where even four-wheel drive vehicles ground to a halt in axle-deep mud.

Today, over ninety per cent of the road is metalled and vast numbers of people travel along it. There are hippies, with little money and no transport, hitching lifts on trucks and buses, packaged holiday makers on professionally organised overland trips and the inevitable bunch of Australians with Kombi vans on their way home. The lords of the road are the big and beefy truck drivers making a handsome livelihood from piloting enormous transporters from one continent to the next.

The vehicles are as diverse as the people who travel in them. Land Rovers, old battered Ford Transits, Bedford trucks, fire engines, ambulances and even double-decker buses. Everything has travelled the road to Kathmandu.

I set out with no experience and few ideas of what the overland journey entailed. Our main requirement was a suitable vehicle and this was sponsored, at no cost to the expedition, by Bristol Street Motors. Fitted out with cloth seats and stereo, and equipped with a giant roof rack, bull bars, sump guards and heavy duty suspension, it was the ideal overlanders' vehicle.

For several weeks after Christmas in 1975, I had pored over maps of Europe and Asia as I traced out a route. At last my hypothetical route was planned, and who better to ask than the Automobile Association's Overseas Advice Centre. I called them in Birmingham and asked the woman at the end of the phone what the road was like out to Kathmandu and which route she would recommend. Her reply was:

'Oh, its easy, just cross the Channel and head east, it's motorway all the way.'

I thought this was a bit optimistic and far from the truth. It wasn't until I had put the phone down that I realised the date – April 1st!

However, good did come from the phone call and within a couple of days a mass of cyclostyled hand-outs and leaflets produced by the AA appeared on my desk. There was everything, ranging from amateur mechanics, what to do in a sandstorm, what to eat and drink and what not to eat and drink, techniques for driving through sand dunes and flood water. Supplementing my reading with books from the local library, I rapidly became conversant with the problems and pitfalls of the overland trip.

Our journey from Frankfurt, down into Austria and across into Yugoslavia was uneventful. The Yugoslavs, for some reason which I failed to understand, suspected us of smuggling sausages of all things. Eventually we managed to convince them that we were bona fide travellers and were allowed to continue our journey.

The three-lane road down through Yugoslavia is fast and dangerous. Wrecks litter the roadside and Turkish migrant workers from the car factories and coal mines of Germany scream south along the centre lane on their way to spend annual holidays with friends and relatives in Turkey. The ancient tranquillity of Greece made a welcome contrast. A few hours' rest, a blissful swim in the Mediterranean and once more on the road.

Then across the Bosphorus to Turkey where Asia begins as Europe ends. We drove into Istanbul and down to the bustling harbour. It is a fascinating place, with ships lining up alongside the quayside for provisioning and porters scurrying from one warehouse to the next and clambering up catwalks to disgorge their enormous loads into empty holds.

Two days out and 700 miles east of Istanbul, disaster struck when the engine seized. A local mechanic was found and we watched pensively as he stripped the motor but even to a layman the bent push rods and broken valves looked serious. With the nearest Ford garage 300 miles back west in Ankara, I hired a flat-topped wagon, loaded the van on to the back of it and Rob Hastings and I began the long trek back to Ankara, leaving the rest of the expedition with all the equipment, camping in a bomb crater in the middle of a cornfield.

Half-joking I shouted out to Mick as we drove off, 'See you in a week.' Little did I realise how true that statement was going to be. Obtaining spare parts was like trying to buy a second-hand Russian Soyuz spacecraft.

'The last time something like this happened,' the man at the Ford garage confided in me, 'it took four weeks to get the parts flown out, two weeks to recover them from customs, and one day to repair the vehicle.'

My plans were shattered. In choosing the overland route to transport equipment and personnel we had taken a calculated risk, but a break-down of this magnitude was catastrophic. The time delay meant we would miss the peak water flow in the river and would possibly have to call the trip off before even launching the canoes.

There was only one thing for it, and that was to get the parts, and get them quickly, even if it meant flying to London, picking them up and flying back again!

A Telex machine was put at my disposal and I contacted Bristol Street Motors. The keyboard operator typed out a cryptic message to George Ellis in Birmingham, listing the parts we required and after a few minutes a reply appeared on the print-out.

'Parts being carried by passenger on Turkish Airlines flight arriving 3.40 am Istanbul tomorrow.' I groaned but acknowledged the Telex and confirmed that we would meet the flight. Somehow I had to get from Ankara to Istanbul, over four hundred miles in ten hours, since by now it was past five pm. Hurriedly we put a call through to the airport. Yes, there was a flight from Ankara to Istanbul at seven pm that evening. Could they check on availability, I asked, and hung on for several minutes until the reservation girl came back to the phone. She regretted but all the seats were taken and there was a waiting list of thirty people.

It had to be a hire car and we anxiously scanned the Turkish version of yellow pages until we found a firm that was still open.

It was a long, hot, punishing drive and we covered the four hundred miles in eight hours, arriving with a few minutes to spare at Istanbul International Airport. We waited as arranged with a Bristol Street sign aloft but, as the last few passengers filtered through, we realised the parts were not on board.

There followed two days of frantic activity. A second Telex somehow managed to find us through the British Embassy in Istanbul, with a new date and time, and this time the parts would be arriving air cargo requiring clearance through customs and excise. Turkish import regulations are some of the most archaic in the world and for two days we tramped from one building to the next, flitting from office to office as papers were signed, stamped, checked and double-checked, until at last we were allowed to import our spares. Late on Friday afternoon they were released fom customs. The garage in Ankara was closed over the weekend and it wasn't until Monday that repairs began. By six pm the mechanic had finished and, keeping our fingers crossed, the battery terminals were connected up and the engine started. At least it worked and we breathed a sigh of relief as the motor idled away. A quick tune up and test run and then off to pick up the rest of the team who were anxiously waiting our return.

They had had a fine time, being fêted and feasted by the local town and treated as celebrities. Dave, who was rapidly becoming proficient in Turkish, had even formed a canoe club on a local pond. With the vehicle loaded and an encouraging cheer from the Manby Canoe Club (Turkish Branch), we set off. Alerted by a strong smell of diesel and a rapidly falling fuel gauge we ground to a halt and inspected the fuel tank. A steady stream of diesel squirted from a one-inch puncture hole in the tank and whilst Mick stuck his finger in the hole and stopped the flow of diesel oil, Rob mixed up some Araldite and, using cotton wool purloined from the medical kit, plugged the hole. Within a few minutes it had set solid.

Turkey has the worst roads imaginable and we nursed the Transit along a hard-packed gravel and rock surface. The sharp flints played havoc with the tyres, slicing into the canvas and causing numerous punctures and delays, as wheels were changed and tubes replaced.

A constant stream of brand new BMWs and Mercedes Benz limousines streaked past us, on their way to the oil-rich state of Iran. At one petrol stop we pulled in to find a BMW over the pits. It was in a fleet of ten cars being driven non-stop from Frankfurt to Teheran and beneath the car was a German student friend of ours.

He told us he had been hired in Frankfurt to drive the car for the equivalent of £200.00. Having delivered the car he would then fly back from Teheran to Germany. He was earning every penny of his money and had been on the go non-stop for four days, to get the cars to eagerly awaiting customers.

There are several high mountain passes in Turkey going up to 11,000 feet. In winter they are often closed by snow but in summer the weather, we found, was stifling hot. Despite having wedged the bonnet open to let more air circulate around the engine, the temperature gauge was edging into the red and we crawled up the highest of the passes in first gear. It was hot and sticky inside the van and by the time we reached the top it was unbearable, as we pulled into the side and tumbled out to admire the exciting view of hills and plains extending to the distant horizon. After a very welcome cooling-off period for man and engine, we raced down the opposite side, with a cool breeze gushing in through open windows.

Crossing from Turkey to Iran, we drove through the bustling city of Teheran late at night and on to roads which were flat, featureless and fast. At night we never ceased to be amused and entertained by the wagons which the drivers decorate with hundreds of brightly-coloured lights so that they look like mobile Christmas trees.

Our first petrol stop was incredible. I left Gosling filling up the fifteen-gallon tank and returned to find everyone armed with notepads and pocket calculators busily computing.

'He's right,' said Gosling.

'What do you mean, he's right?' I queried.

'We couldn't believe the price we've been charged for fuel.'

'You mean he's overcharging?'

'Far from it,' exclaimed John. 'He's just charged us £1.50 for fifteen gallons.'

I just couldn't believe it, with a full tank in England costing over £12.00.

Thirty-six hours later we arrived at the Afghanistan border and began a frustrating six-hour wait, as vehicle after vehicle was scrutinised and meticulously searched for drugs.

At last our turn came and it was only when the small Afghanistan customs officer came to my medical bag that I began to worry. The Afghans impose long prison terms on anyone caught in possession of hashish and other drugs. Foreigners seeming to fare worse than most and as he asked me to open my medical bag, I realised there were ten emergency ampoules of morphine inside. There was nothing I could do as he sifted through the phials and pills. He picked up the morphine and I realised that this could be difficult.

'What's this?' he said.

'Well, actually it's morphine in case anyone breaks a leg,' I replied, and to my surprise he nodded approvingly, put the drugs back and closed the case. I still wonder if he was generously impressed by our wise safety provision or confused by the terminology used. Morphine, after all, is purified hashish. Whichever it was, we were glad to get through the Afghan customs – at last!

An hour to re-load the vehicle and then into the hot dry desert of Afghanistan. A fine tarmac road stretched for miles in front of us. Constructed with Russian aid over fifteen years ago, it has petrol stations every fifty miles and lamp-posts every fifty yards. When they constructed the road, the Russians forgot that there was precious little electricity in Afghanistan. So the electric driven petrol pumps have been converted to hand cranks, and as for the lamp-posts, well, the locals just tether the camels to them.

The last hundred miles to Kabul, which is only a stone's throw from Pakistan, were fraught, because damage and scorching heat made tyre after tyre blow. Although it was a six-wheel Transit with two tyres on either side at the back, we dropped to three tyres at the back, and then two, as we ran out of spares. Limping along at a snail's pace we finally made Kabul, where more tyres were bought. After getting the Transit right, we rested for a day before starting the climb up into the Kabul Gorge to the Pakistan border. Arriving too late to cross the no-man's land from Afghanistan to Pakistan, we slept the night at the border, before crossing the next day.

The Kabul Gorge is a climatic as well as physical barrier between the two countries and we left the hot, dry deserts of Afghanistan and crossed into the torrential rains of Pakistan.

Ten miles outside Lahore we ran into flood water. I was at the wheel and the road was littered with abandoned and swamped cars. Gunning the engine to keep the revs up, I edged into what appeared to be a shallow but as the water started coming in through the windscreen I realised – and it didn't need much imagination to do this – that we were in deep water.

There was no time for panic as I yelled for everyone to get out and start pushing. The engine coughed and spluttered as we inched forward through the brown, muddy ooze. The only way I could tell where the road went under all the slime was for the others to wade along in front. If they sank up to their necks, then I steered well away. We carried on like this for over two hours, negotiating many sections of flooded road, but none as bad as the first. Fields for miles around were flooded, and the locals, marooned in their houses, watched and stared, quite content to wait for the waters to subside.

It came as a relief to leave the flooded lowlands around Lahore, but this relief was short-lived as we came to another major hold up: a wagon had overturned in the centre of the road and we watched in astonishment as the locals, instead of making efforts to right the wagon, just diverted the road around it. Mick Hopkinson claimed the wagon was still there on the way back to England but the diverted road had been tarmaced.

We raced along, intent on reaching Nepal by the end of August. Pakistan was crossed, we sped through India and arrived at the Nepalese border. It was only eighty miles to Kathmandu and we thought we could do it in a couple of hours. It took two and a half days negotiating a road that had been swept away by avalanches and blocked by landslides. Progress was painfully slow and at one point it took us half a day to cover one hundred yards.

At last, exhausted, we rolled into the outer suburbs of Kathmandu. We booked into the Hotel Asia and relaxed in the luxury of hot baths, clean sheets and comfortable beds. I rang Mike Cheney who was handling our arrangements in Nepal and he came down to the hotel with five of his staff, whom we had engaged to work on the expedition. There was Santabier who was to be our chief sirdar, two Panchos, one of whom was acting as second sirdar and the other as cook, and two sixteen year old cook boys, Jimmy and Soupa. In addition we would employ fifty porters who were to be chosen by Santabier.

The next few days were very busy indeed, although it was a relief to have arrived in Kathmandu and at last to have ended the long trek from Frankfurt.

The Nepalese journalists were quite used to people who wanted to climb on Everest, but the wish to canoe on Everest caused the usual surprise. However to their credit, they were very kind and they did know about the Dudh Kosi which was something of an advance.

Red-tape and bureaucracy thrive in all countries, whatever their climate or state of development. Nepal is no exception, it has its fair share of both; more than its fair share if our experience was anything to go by. Consequently we had to spend a considerable time sitting around or standing in queues, patiently waiting for officials.

The delay did give some of the party the chance to get the flavour of a city that is an intriguing mixture of the old, medieval and new. The new means provisions for the tourist trade.

At 1600 hours on August 30th, 1977 our expedition finally

received the necessary documents with the minister's seal of approval. I hope that he also approved the vigorous manner in which we joined in the local festivities. That night the city was alight and alive with rejoicing and our party was appropriately inspired.

5

The Walk in to Pheriche

TUESDAY, AUGUST 31ST. The alarm clock shrilled me into wakefulness and I reached out and fumbled to turn it off. It clattered to the floor and was silenced indefinitely as its glass shattered into a thousand pieces. I turned over and buried my head in the sheets, delaying a few moments longer before the inevitable start of another day.

I rolled out of bed, showered, packed my sack and manhandled it down to the hotel lobby and outside into the cold grey of dawn. Mike Cheney was sitting patiently at the wheel of his brick-red Land Rover station wagon. Two of his sherpa staff were busily loading the roof up with rucksacks, bags of rice for the porters and large aluminium cooking pots.

It was only six am and we were all feeling hungover from the previous evening's festivities. At last we were ready to go and I clambered aboard Cheney's Land Rover as he gunned the engine and we rolled forward.

The streets of Kathmandu were strangely deserted as we passed through the outer suburbs heading north towards Lamosangu from where we would begin the 180-mile walk to Base Camp Everest. Cheney, bright and cheery, enjoying himself enormously with yet another expedition under way, was chatting in Nepali to Purna, his personal cook boy, who was sitting astride the Land Rover gearstick. We passed through a check point and Mike Cheney, instantly recognised, was waved through with only cursory glances at our trekking permits.

We arrived at Lamosangu by ten am. For the last few miles we had wound along the banks of the Sun Kosi River. It looked a formidable river with rapids very similar to those on the Colorado in the USA, with fifteen-foot standing waves and colossal holes and stoppers. At Lamosangu there is a large suspension bridge, the only crossing point for many hundreds of miles.

Eventually the Sun Kosi heads east, picking up many subsidiary rivers including our own Dudh Kosi draining off the Himalayas, and joins up with the Arun River and empties out into the vast plains of India.

Across the bridge on the far bank there was a splurge of colour; reds, blues, oranges as our porters sorted out their loads of canoes, tents, food boxes and all the other expedition paraphernalia we needed. The Land Rover was rapidly unloaded and we cautiously crossed the racing brown muddy waters of the Sun Kosi.

John Liddell pulled out his spring balance and began weighing the porters' loads. They had agreed to carry sixty pounds and John was determined to see each had his full quota. Meanwhile John Gosling was busy cutting four-foot squares of orange fluorescent plastic sheeting which we were giving to the porters to protect them from the rain. They acted like small children at Christmas, crowding around, pushing and jostling and snatching as each sheet was cut. What a chaotic sight! There were porters and boxes scattered all over the field. Would we ever see our cherished gear and possessions again?

I decided to leave John Liddell to sort out the loads and sat in the shade of a dry stone wall and watched at a distance as individual porters were loaded up and headed for the Everest trail. A big crowd of gawping dirty children had gathered. They were fascinated and intrigued by the canoes. A small smiling boy sat in one of the canoes, John Gosling gave him a paddle, someone put a crash helmet on his head and then everyone was laughing and joking and cameras were clicking to capture the scene. How many times the same departure scene had been re-enacted as mountaineering expeditions left for Sola Khumbu and Everest and its satellite peaks, I asked myself. But this time our expedition was different. We were going to Everest to canoe, not to climb it. Our porters explained to the locals we were going canoeing not climbing. They seemed totally bemused and confused.

We had fifty-six porters, Tamangs not Sherpas from the

lower Sun Kosi Valley. There were men and women, young boys and girls. The males were dressed in tattered shorts and loose-fitting shirts, the women draped in black cloths wound around their torsos. They all walked barefoot, their hardened soles protecting them from razor-sharp rocks and flints on the trail.

They carry their loads using a headstrap with necks flexed and gazing downwards. Two cords run from the headstrap to the load which is carried on their backs. The thirteen and a half foot, thirty-pound canoes were carried in the same way, held broadside on to their backs with string running from either end up to a wide headband across their forehead. After some argument, John Liddell, who had now fully taken over the job of organising the porters, finally agreed to classify the canoes as ice-fall ladders, since they were long, awkward and difficult to manage, and pay the twelve porters carrying them twenty pence a day extra. Our remaining porters were being paid sixty pence a day which is almost in the supertax bracket by Nepalese standards.

Our chief sirdar, Santabier, was supervising operations. Quiet, efficient, speaking broken English, he is one of the professional trekkers, making an excellent living from the increased popularity of trekking and tourism in Nepal.

By mid-morning, all were ready to move. We only had framed rucksacks to carry containing our personal possessions. Mike Cheney shook hands, wished us well and waved us off. He watched wistfully as we began the tortuous ascent up the beginnings of the Everest trail, no doubt wishing he was many years younger and able to come along and join in our adventure.

It was stifling hot and the sun shone down through a brilliant blue sky. I was sweating profusely as I wandered alone up the trail. The soil was hard packed from the compression of many feet and the leather of my new boots creaked as I plodded slowly upwards. In the distance someone was singing a Nepalese folk song and now, way down in the valley, smoke from Lamosangu was curling its way up into the sky and the daily bus from Kathmandu was hooting its horn as it rattled into town.

It was a time for relaxation. Freed from the perpetual problems and worries which had beset the expedition since leaving England, I now had nothing to do but amble along, marvelling at the beauty of the Nepalese countryside. I began to plan our descent. Would it be too late to go up to Base Camp and still catch the monsoon rains further down river? Would we arrive to find the river no more than a pile of boulders? These were some of the questions I asked myself.

At last, the summit of the first hill. Mick Hopkinson, John Gosling and Roger Huyton were there with a glass of *chi* already waiting. It was hot, thirsty work; I collapsed in the shade of the teahouse. A map of the approach march was laid out on the table and we studied it closely.

We discussed the walk in. From leaving Kathmandu to reaching the Dudh Kosi valley is approximately a hundred miles and from Jubing, which is the point at which the approach march crosses the river to Base Camp, is a further eighty miles. The trail must cross many river valleys since it heads east and all the river valleys drain north-south. It's a regular routine of dropping into a valley and then climbing out, so that by the time the trail reaches the Dudh Kosi River, you have been up and down 44,000 feet, yet are only 300 feet higher than when at Kathmandu. This is all rather discouraging, particularly for someone such as myself who finds walking from one ward in the hospital to the next is a long way! As Mick Hopkinson appropriately described the walk in, 'It's a bit like climbing Ben Nevis before breakfast, Ben Nevis after breakfast and a quick Ben Nevis before you stop for the night.'

We pressed on. It was a strange and fascinating experience: the woodsmoke-filled teahouses, the smoke filtering its way out through the roofs, the children racing along behind us excitedly chattering away, the grizzled old men and women sitting in the dark recesses of doorways and watching yet another expedition passing through. By four that afternoon, it was a deluge and the path became a gushing stream of brown, liquid mud. Weaving our way from one side of the path to the other, trying to avoid the worst of the flooding, we slithered, slipped and swore as we raced for the nearest *chi* house. We huddled inside, a steaming mass of bodies and warmed ourselves with pints of hot, sweet tea.

As quickly as it had begun the rain ceased and we pushed on. The sky was overcast with heavy, cotton-wool clouds hanging overhead and an ominous rumbling of thunder in the distance. We pitched camp and the cooks busied themselves lighting the fire, for all our food had to be cooked on open wood fires.

The canoes were translucent and seemed to glow when the sun caught them but they were very awkward for the porters to carry, because they were too long to be held in a vertical position up their backs and so, instead, they stuck out horizontally six feet or so on either side. Every time the path narrowed or twisted round a sharp corner the men had to manoeuvre with great circumspection in order not to get the boats knocked off their heads or bashed up on projecting trees or rocks. Sometimes the porters had to twist and turn sideways, snaking to and fro, in order to edge themselves and their loads round steep bends. Up and down the hills, heads bent forward, backs rounded, the tamangs plodded steadily on. They would struggle into camp at the end of the day, sometimes in groups, sometimes alone, stack their loads beneath a large tarpaulin and, looking wet and bedraggled, they would disappear rapidly off to the nearest village to find food and shelter for the night.

Soaked by the deluge, the wood was difficult to light and it took some time for Pancho the cook to coax some life into the fire. I sat watching from the tent door as he puffed and blew at the base of the fire, going pillar-box red in the face and almost looking as though he was going to blow up.

Someone suggested going to the local *chang* house. We wandered across the field we had camped in, picking our way around massive piles of cow dung. It was dark by the time dinner was ready and we weaved our way back to the frame tent where Pancho was ladling out the meal.

We ate in silence – Batchelor's dehydrated stew, Cadbury's Smash and peas, followed by Mars Bars, washed down with lashings of steaming hot tea.

Mick Hopkinson, standing centre, and the team shelter in a wayside teahouse as the rain beats down.

Canoes at Everest Base Camp, ready for the altitude challenge.

The avalanche above Tengpoche monastery.

Looking up the inaccessible reaches of the Dudh Kosi valley.

I had only taken a few mouthfuls when someone said they thought they could taste fibre-glass in the food. Someone else said they could as well, and then everyone could taste fibre-glass in the food! The stew, the potatoes, the peas, even the Mars Bars tasted of fibre-glass resin! And the tea, well, that tasted of soap!

We sat discussing the problem and concluded that all those days lying about in the sun in Turkey had caused the fibre-glass resin to evaporate and the smell had pervaded the food containers which were stacked around it. We checked the food box. There was a strong smell of fibre-glass and the bars of soap had melted.

'Oh well, there's nothing we can do about it. I only hope it's not too bad in the other boxes,' I remarked.

The meal over, people slowly left and drifted back to their own tents. I was sharing a tent with Roger and we had come prepared with a cassette player, pre-recorded cassettes and, of course, several bottles of vodka from our Warrington sponsor. As Roger said after our first day's carry, 'We might as well drink it as carry it.' I drifted off into a drugged, alcoholic sleep to the strains of Dylan blaring out on the cassette.

All too soon it was dawn and at six am the next morning the tent flap was unzipped and Jimmy, the assistant cook, looking bright and cheerful, thrust two steaming pint mugs of tea inside. I never like early rising and, cocooned inside my sleeping bag, I pulled it further over my head, trying to snatch a few more minutes' sleep. No such luck! Within five minutes two porters were stamping outside the tent door waiting for us to vacate it, so that they could collapse it and get on their way. I tumbled out of the tent door, spilt half my mug of tea and gulped down the remainder before that too was spilt.

It was a cold, damp dawn and the sun was only just beginning to filter through a dense bank of grey cloud in the east. Rucksacks packed, we straggled after the porters, spending the first hour climbing and then began the steady drop down into a wide river valley.

The walk in to Everest, or for that matter any other Himalayan peak, rapidly takes on a routine. Waking at six am you have a cup of *chi*, pack your small rucksack and then off. Three hours' walking and stop for breakfast of hot pancakes, porridge and Ryvita biscuits with a generous covering of margarine and marmalade, and giant mugs of tea. Then off again with frequent stops for tea and *chang*. But no midday break and no midday meal. The sun beat down incessantly during the morning and early afternoon. By three pm the heavy monsoon clouds had appeared and by four pm it was deluging down again. Umbrellas which were used as sunshades in the morning came into their own, offering some resistance to the solid sheets of water as the skies opened in the afternoon.

Soon after four pm, whenever we were near a village with a good camp-site, we would stop for the night. The porters would slope off to the shops, tents would be put up and we would drink *chang* and make stilted conversation with the locals, whilst our evening meal was being cooked. Then off to bed to read and talk, write up diaries and letters home.

I was tied up with *All the President's Men* by Carl Bernstein and Bob Woodward. It is a tremendous piece of investigative writing and, reading with the light from a flickering candle, I was getting deeper and deeper into the scandal and intrigue. Could Nixon really have not known about Watergate until such a late date? Who were the 'fall' guys and who were the guilty ones? I found it fascinating as the plot unravelled itself and resolved to see the film when I got home.

We became fitter as we walked. I had started 1976 off totally unfit, having had a serious bout of glandular fever complicated by hepatitis. In January and February I had worked hard to regain my strength but from mid-March until we left in July, I had found it increasingly difficult to take time off for canoe training and eventually resigned myself to trying to tone up my muscles with one hour of squash a day on the hospital squash court. With my 'bleeper' in the corner of the court and telephone outside the door, I could play squash whilst being on call.

The walk was not without problems. Food was a constant source of contention and the fibre-glass arguments reached the size of the Watergate issue. There were two camps: those that could positively identify it in the food and those that could not but said it was a figment of the imagination. Gradually more and more people abandoned the latter camp until only John Gosling, who had spent so much time and effort organising the food and had manfully been trying to persuade everyone that there was nothing wrong with it, finally had to admit there was fibre-glass but professed to like it. The porridge seemed to be affected more than anything else and our cook appeared unable to gauge how much would be eaten, so that invariably there would be ample second and third helpings. Only Roger, John Gosling and Mick Hopkinson seemed to be able to tackle large quantities. Whilst we sat back and watched, they would have porridge-eating contests, guzzling bowl after bowl after bowl. Roger invariably won: his best was ten large bowls running.

Leeches were a big problem. Many tourists and trekkers walk to Base Camp Everest and in October and November there are throngs of trekkers heading towards Sola Khumbu and the Everest region. At this time of year it is dry and there are very few leeches around.

In September, the weather is wet and warm and the leech abounds. They drop on to the unwary from trees and catch on to exposed thighs and calves from blades of grass. Once on the body, they go unnoticed since they freeze the skin with a local anaesthetic. They fix themselves on with a sucker and series of tentacles and suck blood, getting bigger and bigger by the minute. They get everywhere – into tents, canoeing gear, into boats and even into your underpants which, as one member of the team will testify, is a fate worse than death!

The quickest way to remove the leech is to burn it off with a cigarette. A slower way is to sprinkle salt over it, which has an osmotic effect and makes the leech explode in a bright red mass of blood. Invariably, when removed the leech leaves a bleeding wound, since it also injects an anti-coagulant which stops the blood clotting. These wounds rapidly become infected and were to prove a great problem in the latter part of the expedition.

We rapidly became neurotic about the leech. Everyone had their own ideas on how to defeat the problem, which ranged from walking with plastic bags on your feet to putting salt down your socks and smearing every inch of skin with insect repellent. None worked!

The worst problem was at night. Of all possible bed partners the leech must surely rank as the most unattractive, even downright disagreeable. Numerous devices and techniques were developed to ensure this did not happen. My own preference was to conduct a thorough leech survey of the tent, strip off and do a whole body count for leeches, seal the zips of the tent with carpet tape and then imbibe enough alcohol to act as a hypnotic and allay my fears of attack.

The first test run of my newly-developed and much publicised fool-proof technique was a disaster! Within half an hour I had already suffered a two-prong attack by a pair of leeches. Confident that this was no more than a teething problem with my technique, I slipped off into a light sleep. Suddenly I knew I was finished, as I came to with a jolt and saw a patch of bright red blood, more than a foot in diameter, over the lower part of the sleeping bag. Screaming in terror and imagining I was bleeding to death, I ripped the bag off and searched madly with a pen-light torch for the culprit. It just wasn't there and recovering the inner bag from the corner of the tent, where I had thrown it in panic, that too was searched. I burst out laughing and to my eternal embarrassment realised what had happened. The so-called patch of blood was no more than several feet of bright red tape which had come unstuck from the zipper.

Five days' walking had put us halfway to the river. We were all much fitter and beginning to enjoy the walk, absorbing the sights, smell and sounds of the Nepalese scenery. A competitive instinct developed amongst the team members and we pushed ourselves to stay out in front and be the first to the top of the inevitable 10,000 or 11,000 feet shoulders we had to scale to climb out of one valley and into the next.

September 6th, my twenty-fifth birthday, dawned bright and clear. We walked along the valley floor until three hours brought us to a small village and the start of the inevitable climb. The heat was oppressive. Stripped to the waist, we sat in the shade of a *chi* house and swatted flies as we waited for breakfast. Leo's girlfriend, Barbara, produced a can of McEwans beer to celebrate my birthday but by the time it had been passed round and shared between twelve thirsty people, we barely managed a mouthful each.

Things were going well. We were still getting the monsoon rain which was so important to ensure that the river was running high and the team members were beginning to know each other; old friendships strengthened and new ones developed.

Expeditions are very closed communities. You forget the outside world, its problems and your problems and become ensconced in your own little expedition world. It is a time to reflect, look back on your life before and look forward to the future.

We had no set jobs to do and would spend the day wandering along the trail, stopping at *chi* and *chang* houses, taking a diversion from the trail to go through a Nepalese village, or simply enjoying the unique scenery.

Leo and Mick Reynolds were occupied with shooting as much footage as possible of the walk in. Occasionally they set up pre-arranged sequences but mostly they would race ahead and get shots as we struggled in.

Leo has a tremendous ability to keep on going, the true sign of a professional, since after a hard day's walking you are only too happy to collapse on a Karrimat and dream the rest of the day away, whilst Leo would be seen hurrying backwards and forwards, racing up hillocks, cameras whirring and clicking all the time as he tried to capture the progress of the expedition on film.

On the 9th we reached the Dudh Kosi River. I recorded the event in my diary.

> We stopped for lunch at 11.30 a.m. above the Dudh Kosi valley and gulped down pancakes with Ryvitas and jam, then started out to drop down to the river. The sun filtered through a dense canopy of foliage as we jumped and raced our way down the rock-strewn trail.

The most exciting point of any expedition is when the objective first comes into view and we rounded the last bluff, suddenly to emerge no more than thirty feet above the swirling waters of the Dudh Kosi, racing under the bridge at over 30 mph. It looks very technical with many stoppers and partly submerged rocks. It's going to be very easy to write canoes off. What surprises me most is that it is so sustained – the breakouts are there but will require some very precise canoeing to make sure we get them. There is little chance of swimming out of the river if you do fall out of your canoe. Leo wanted us to shoot the fall above the iron suspension bridge which spans the river and breaks out below, but I persuaded him it was impractical as it would be almost impossible to portage the canoes back up to the trail from our stopping point, as the river banks are almost vertical. I expect I was just shying away from committing myself on an extremely difficult section of rapids without any build-up.

We grabbed a few shots and crossed the high swaying steel bridge to the far bank, where a grand confrontation between Santabier and the rest of the porters seemed to be in full swing. Apparently, they wanted to stop a hundred yards upstream at the river crossing town of Jubing, whereas Santabier was urging them to press on as far as the much larger village of Kharikhola, where there was a better camping area and a schoolhouse in which we could reorganise our porter loads.

Eventually Santabier's decision stood and we pushed on out of the gorge upstream towards Kharikhola. It was a very steep ascent and as we climbed, the Dudh Kosi valley opened up in front of us. The river above Jubing is in a steep-sided gorge and looked dicey canoeing territory, with the gorge walls rising hundreds of feet, almost sheer from the river bed, making portaging difficult if not impossible. If a canoeist wishes to say that he has descended the whole of a river, then theoretically he is meant to stay in the river bed when portaging. But here we might have to climb up the rocky sides with ropes, haul the canoes up after us, walk along the mountain path and then abseil down again to the river bed.

Sweating profusely, we climbed over one thousand feet and panted laboriously up the last few yards of the incline. From now on we would be heading up into the mountains.

Deep in thought, my feet suddenly went from under me and I felt myself fall through space. I cried out in terror as I fell, but in a split second was brought to a spine-jarring halt. Gripped and frightened, I carefully twisted round and looked up to see my rucksack, from which I was suspended, caught in a large branch of a tree. Ten feet above was the path and beneath my boots was fifty feet of space.

Rog had been following and seen my unplanned descent. He called down, 'Hold it, while I get a few pictures.'

'Never mind the bloody pictures,' I replied, 'just get me out of here.'

Five minutes later, dishevelled and pale faced, I was heaved back on to the trail. It had been a close shave and we hadn't even been on the river when it happened!

We arrived at Kharikhola, which is a small collection of houses and teashops. There were many children and we sat drinking *chi* in the schoolhouse with hordes of inquisitive youngsters peering at us through chinks in the walls.

That evening the porters drank and feasted late into the night and I drifted off to sleep to the sound of singing and chanting, with the steady beat of drums in the background.

The morning of the 10th dawned bright and clear. For once there had been no overnight rain and the turf outside the tent was dry and springy. Hang-overs abounding from the previous evening's celebrations, the porters were slow in getting under way. John Liddell was once again at loggerheads with his portering staff. We had been laying off porters as we walked in. As food was consumed, fewer boxes were needed to transport it. The previous evening, we had decided to leave ten food boxes and two canoes at Kharikhola, arranging to store these in a *chi* house and paying the Nepalese owner a small fee for looking after their safety. John worked out that we had thirty-six loads, but forty-one porters and was in a heated argument with Santabier, who refused to sack any more of his men.

Eventually a compromise was reached and everyone seemed happy.

It was almost eight am by the time things were sorted out and we were just setting out from camp when Joyce Tabbner, who was crossing a single-plank bridge over the gushing waters of a mountain stream which ran through the village, slipped and was deposited in a most unladylike fashion in the icy cold water. She sat there in the middle of the freezing stream, looking so woebegone that unchivalrous lot that we were, although not intending to be unsympathetic, we all burst out laughing. All except Geoff her husband; he was not at all amused. He rushed over to help the recumbent Joyce, for he wasn't at all diverted by our amusement or Joyce's predicament.

Above Kharikhola the Dudh Kosi valley stretched out in front of us. It is a steeply-cut river valley and far in the distance we could see the Himalayan snow-capped peaks whose melt water formed our river.

We followed the river valley upwards, on the trail which wound its way along the steep and precipitous valley sides, never very far from but many thousand feet above the streak of water below. Past Luglha, the mountain airstrip where dollar rich American tourists fly in to view Everest, and then we began to drop down to the river.

At Phakding we crossed the Dudh Kosi once again, and now we would be walking along within a few yards of the river.

There was a constant flow of people travelling between Namche Bazar, the market town for Sola Khumbu and the surrounding countryside. We camped that night by the side of the river. The noise was deafening, and sitting on the banks we could hear rocks and boulders being trundled and rolled along the river bed.

We were all keen to get back into action on the water and whilst Leo rushed backwards and forwards erecting tripods and choosing angles, we unloaded our canoes and changed into canoeing gear. I donned swimming trunks and wet-suit trousers, a Damart thermal vest, lightweight anorak, a lifejacket and canoeing helmet.

We surveyed the short quarter of a mile section of river as

we walked up alongside it. It looked difficult canoeing with large stoppers and breaking waves.

I forced my way through the scrub on the banks of the river and launched my boat into the Dudh Kosi for a trial run. Carefully I fitted the neoprene spraysheet around the cockpit to seal me inside and make the join between me and the boat completely watertight. It felt good to be back in the water again after such a long absence. I pushed off into the current and was immediately spun around and swept off downstream. A quick break-out and I sat in the eddy behind a rock, waiting for the rest of the team to get afloat.

Everyone was looking rather shaky. Big water paddling normally requires a long build-up on smaller rapids and yet here we were, about to tackle the biggest water we had seen for a long time, without having been in a canoe for two months.

Mick Hopkinson edged in beside me and we sat silently waiting for the signal from Leo that the cameras were ready to turn. We were all gripped up.

At last it came.

Instantaneous release of adrenalin and explosion of power as the canoe edges into the current. It sweeps around and we're off at over thirty mph. I ride wave after wave using the few seconds the canoe is on the crest of the wave to alter direction. Edge to the left to miss a stopper, to the right to miss a partly submerged rock. In front, Mick goes over and I try to keep an eye on him whilst trying to slow the canoe down and get a line down the rapids. A wave crashes down on top of me, and then another and I drop into a stopper. I brace hard on the face of it and paddle along the wall of white water until, after what seems like a lifetime, I finally find a run-out.

Mick seems to be in trouble and suddenly his canoe stands vertically in the water as he loops in a stopper. I lean hard over and try and edge the canoe away but the water is too heavy and the canoe fails to respond, as Mick's canoe comes crashing down on top of me. And then I'm over. No time for fear. No time to get a breath of air. The cold is intense and automatically the paddles go into the eskimo-roll position, a sweep, a press and the canoe rights itself. Air, I fill my lungs and frantically search for an eddy. One looms up on the left bank and I paddle desperately for it. So does Mick and we both hit the backwash together.

We were both gasping for breath. My lungs were near to bursting point and even at 8,000 feet the lack of oxygen was critical. My arms were like lead, and I could hardly lift the paddle. We had all been taken in by the notoriously deceptive speed and size of the rapids. Of course, Leo had loved every minute of it. We shot beneath the bridge with the locals shouting and clapping their hands together in excitement.

We manhandled the canoes on to the right-hand bank and Leo came dashing down, full of praise. 'That was great, lads, it looked really impressive. I missed some of it, though. Could you do it again?' The air was blue as Mick Hopkinson told Leo what to do.

That night we talked late after supper. We had all been surprised by the speed and gradient. It left very little time to think and no time for mistakes. None of the team had been on rapids which were as continuous and sustained as those of the Dudh Kosi. Normally a rapid is followed by a section of flat water. The Dudh Kosi was one continuous rapid, where to fall out of your canoe would be disastrous with little chance of swimming out of the white water.

Leaving the porters to dismantle the camp site we left early the next morning to continue walking up the Dudh Kosi to its source, looking at the river with renewed intensity, making mental notes of waterfalls and the right line down the rapids.

To a canoeist, a river poses a series of water hazards or problems. Just as a rock climber looks at a rock face and picks a line up it, in a similar way the canoeist must decide on a line down a section of rapids. He must decide whether he is going to miss a stopper, edge his canoe past or take his luck with an exploding wave.

As we walked upstream it was, as we feared, continuous rapids. There was no let up, and no respite, with most of the rapids touching on grade six, the hardest there is. No chance of swimming out of a grade six spill.

That night we made Namche Bazar. I seemed to have

picked up a virus and was feeling desperately ill and totally drained. I struggled up the long climb to Namche, stopping every few minutes to rest and was only halfway up when Mick Hopkinson came bounding back down the trail. He had been to the top, seen me in difficulties and dropped back down to help. I gratefully handed my pack over and Mick helped me up the last 300 feet to Namche. It was a wonderful gesture on Mick's part as he was probably equally tired but it demonstrated the strong team spirit which was developing.

Namche was shrouded in mist as we arrived. It is the market town for the whole of the Sola Khumbu area and is very prosperous, made so only in recent years from the vast amount of trade it does with trekkers, tourists and expeditions on their way to Everest and the surrounding Himalayan peaks.

It has a wonderful collection of shops with shelves stacked high with the left-overs from the numerous expeditions which pass through the village every year. It is just as easy to buy canned Heinz baked beans or a Dundee cake in Namche as it is in a Sainsbury's store in Birmingham. We found delicacies we had not seen for months and had a feast, gorging ourselves until we could eat no more.

We slept that night at the Footrest Hotel. I found it amazing how the Sherpas open up their houses and take great sacrifices to make virtual strangers feel at home. We were ushered into a large circular room up a rickety flight of stairs. A fire was burning fiercely in the centre and the smoke was drifting lazily through small slit windows high in the walls and chinks in the slate roof.

Arranged around the fire in a circular fashion in tiers were hard wooden benches, and we emptied our rucksacks out to dry sleeping bags and air mouldy and damp clothes.

The owner's wife was busily preparing *rhaksi*, a highly potent drink produced by distilling *chang* and we watched and sampled the throat-burning liquid as it was distilled.

Tonight we were eating local food, and plates piled high with rice and highly-spiced *dahl* were produced. We drank and talked late into the night and slipped off into a drugged sleep.

Bleary eyed, we were up again at six am. Breakfast was *tsampi* mixed into a porridge with tea and margarine added, so that it was rather like a baby cereal, and then we were off again to check in with the police and have our permits stamped to head on up into the Everest Massif.

All expeditions to Everest have to have official government approval and our own permits were closely scrutinised by the police chief. Alas, all was not in order, since the writing on Mike Reynolds' permit had been washed out by the rain. More delays, more arguments and eventually a radio call to Kathmandu, to check the list of members of the expedition lodged with the Minister of Foreign Affairs and we were on our way again.

I was worried about John Liddell as we climbed out of the basin in which Namche is built. His knee was heavily bandaged and he was in considerable pain as we hiked up the steep incline. He was covered in psoriasis and the endless rain and damp had turned his sores septic. To add to his problems he was suffering from an attack of dysentery and limping along, resting on a walking stick, it was all he could do to keep going. John held the record for needing to relieve himself, at one point having to plunge into the bushes twenty-six times before breakfast. Of course the loo paper ran out and when John got back to England and was asked for his thoughts on the expedition, he paused for comment and then said, 'Well, you get to be an expert on big leaves.'

Above Namche once again the river disappeared into a wild and rugged gorge. As we walked we caught odd glimpses of churning white water. At one point, a giant chockstone, as big as three houses, weighing many hundreds of tons, was wedged precariously fifty feet above the river from bank to bank. Was it likely to fall at any moment? Just as we canoed underneath, perhaps?

Further upstream, a small promontory afforded an unhindered view into the gorge and I scrambled on to it to look down from over a thousand feet up on the river below. The banks were covered in dense green jungly vegetation which looked impenetrable.

We pressed on. In front we could see the sun glinting on

the Everest View Hotel, built by some enterprising Japanese businessmen, so that tourists can fly direct from Kathmandu to the hotel's air-strip, and with tanks of oxygen on their backs, stay in the five-star accommodation and sit in the sun lounge, hoping for a view of Everest through a window in the clouds.

We arrived at Tengpoche monastery late that afternoon. Leaving the porters to pitch the tents and prepare the evening meal, I walked down to Pangpoche bridge where the Dudh Kosi drops twenty feet or so into a narrow chasm. Over the years the churning water has scalloped recesses and fashioned underwater caves. I stood on the bridge and watched the water as it was compressed between the vertical rock faces. It swirled and twisted, banking and rolling in endless foam, whipping itself into eddies and whirlpools. With any luck we would be coming through this stretch of water within the week.

In the gathering dusk I retraced my footsteps and climbed back up to the monastery to eat rice and *dahl* and bargain with the monks for climbing gear.

We were up early the next morning. Most expeditions normally rest at the monastery for two or three days and acclimatise. We were running desperately late and, instilled with a sense of urgency, we pressed on, dropping down to the bridge at Pangpoche and then criss-crossing the river, as we headed up to Pheriche at 14,000 feet, where we arrived at two pm.

Pheriche is little more than a collection of stone buildings and we settled down in a *chang* house to idle the afternoon away. It is a barren, desolate place and nowadays the villagers make a living out of tourists, who stop off on their way to Base Camp Everest. For thirty pence a night they are offered floor space in the smoky sherpa huts.

There are three shops stacked full of tinned goods and delicacies, purchased or purloined from expeditions and sold at exorbitant prices to eager tourists. I reflected that our distinctive 'fibre-glass brands' would be easy to distinguish, if they ever did make it on to the shelves.

Here new potatoes were in abundance and were not frowned upon as they were lower down the Everest trail, where everyone ate rice and potatoes were second best. They were delicious, lightly salted, with margarine.

We ate well and whilst I was munching away, I suddenly thought that I would change the plans. It was an impulsive, instantaneous decision made on the spur of the moment. I'm no Chris Bonington, I just play it by ear. It had been a long walk up the Dudh Kosi so far and it had looked a long and difficult descent. Time was limited so we would have to hurry. It didn't look to me, however, as though the river had sufficient water in it to cover the rocky bed for much further up: it was an almost vertical jet of fine spray above Pheriche which looked very shallow. I still hoped to canoe from the Khumbu Glacier lake but it now seemed unlikely that we would be able to launch the canoes between the lake and Pheriche. Despite this, we would still have a very tight schedule to fit in. The best answer to me seemed to be to split the expedition into two. Mick Hopkinson and I would go up to Everest Base Camp and from there to the lake with second cameraman, Mick Reynolds, and our climbers, Eric Jones and Geoff Tabbner, to support us and to take photographs of us at the highest altitude yet attained by canoeists. Meanwhile, the rest of the team would start canoeing down from Pheriche with Leo.

When I announced my new decision it was clearly not popular. Not surprisingly, everyone had hoped to see Mount Everest and to say that they had been to Everest Base Camp. To come within fifteen miles and then not to visit such a famous place was hard. I thought that everyone would see my decision to go to the Base Camp myself as a selfish one but this was not what annoyed them most. The main argument which broke out, and which was the first serious disagreement of the expedition, was whether we should take both Eric and Geoff up with us to Khumbu or not. Rob's party would probably have more use for a climber in the steep gorges above Namche than we would high on the Everest glacier. The canoeists might well need rescuing from difficulty in a tight situation and only a climber would be able to get down the face of vertical rock to help them if they were stuck in a gorge. Leo had said, and I had agreed, that both Geoff and Eric should go up to Base

78

Camp but now the others wanted Geoff with them. Geoff nobly offered to step down. Geoff, who had done so much of the donkey work and the hard grind, had seen Everest as the highlight of his own trip, but he forewent the experience in order to help the rest of the team at Pheriche.

With Mick and I canoeing, Mick Reynolds and Eric in support on the lake and the rest beginning their descent, we had an equal distribution of climbing and canoeing talent and could be confident of success. We of the Base Camp party hoped to attain our altitude record on the lake, then we would check whether or not the upper reaches of the Dudh Kosi were navigable above Pheriche and if they were not, we would hurry on down to join up with the others. In this way the river would be covered at greater speed and in the time available.

Muttering, individuals drifted away from the main eating area and by nine pm everyone was in bed. It was a cold, uncomfortable night. The higher we went, the colder it became and the more we suffered from piles and diarrhoea. I slept fitfully against a background of bellowing yaks.

6

An Altitude Record

WE WERE UP AT six thirty am and off by eight. It was good to be away from the crowd and Mick and I plodded steadily uphill bound for Gorak Shep, Lobuche and Base Camp.

We would have to be extremely careful in choosing our first launching spot on the upper reaches of the Dudh Kosi, for we only had twelve craft and the river was faster than I had expected, the waterfalls were steeper, the rapids more dangerous and there were far more jagged rocks uncovered sticking out ready to snag the canoes. The monsoon rains had unleashed a seething torrent; any canoe slammed against one of those giant boulders would be split in half in a second. We would have to treat this river with great respect.

Of course Geoff wanted to go up to Base Camp and for that matter so did everyone else. But if we were to succeed, it was essential that we work as a team and forget our own personal hopes and ambitions, thinking more of the good of the expedition as a whole. Success was for canoes to have achieved the world altitude record and for canoes to have come down the highest river in the world, not for every-one of us to have done it.

Mick and I walked together talking. I found it hard going. I had only managed to snatch a few hours' sleep the previous night, being troubled by violent bouts of diarrhoea and having to make mad rushes from the tent into the bitterly cold night air. Besides, I was also feeling the effects of altitude and every few hundred yards would come to a rest leaning heavily on my paddle.

The previous evening, John Liddell and I had spent over two hours trying to sort our portering situation out. We had left Kathmandu with fifty-six porters and by the time we left Kharikhola had scaled numbers down to twenty-seven,

Leo Dickinson filming from an aerial rope 200 feet above the canoeists' heads.

Our cook team huddle round the cooking pot to keep warm.

since we had eaten up several food boxes, as well as leaving a cache of provisions and canoes in the schoolhouse at Kharikhola.

By the time we reached Pheriche, we calculated we had twenty-seven porters but only nineteen loads, which at first had me extremely perplexed, until I scrutinised the porters' loads as they came into the camp. I found that some of the 'loads' were no more than a few of the porters' blankets and bags of rice, which they normally carried in addition to our sixty-pound load. Eventually we reached a compromise, dismissed another four porters and carried on with twenty-three.

We were all struggling with the altitude. As most people could only get away from their jobs for three months at the longest, that was the time I had allowed for the whole expedition and I had decided at the outset that it would be more advantageous for us to perfect our canoeing skills by practising on the way out, in Austria and Switzerland, than to spend time sitting around in Nepal getting acclimatised. I had thought that the slow, steady walk up to the base of Everest would in itself accustom us to altitude, as we were already physically fit.

But now, dizzy and numb, breathing heavily, I realised that I might well have been wrong. To break out of a stopper requires tremendous physical effort and, as I struggled to keep up with the others, I wondered if I would ever manage some of those walls of water I'd seen on the Dudh Kosi.

At 14,200 feet the air is rarefied to the extent that if you are not sufficiently well acclimatised, as we were not, the calf and thigh muscles rapidly develop cramp and every step requires a major effort. Most people who climb Everest spend two or three days at Tengpoche to get used to the altitude but we had come straight through.

At ten thirty we halted for breakfast. It was a cold, bleak place and a solitary hut stood by the banks of the gushing mountain torrent. There was no firewood since we were now well above the tree line and the second sirdar, Pancho, who had taken charge of our four porters, argued and bartered for wood with a tuberculous and choleric-looking

Sherpa who appeared in the doorway of the shack. Eventually they struck a bargain and shook hands. Within a few minutes we were sitting sheltered from the wind to the leeward side of the hut, with the kettle simmering away and pancakes sizzling on the hot iron.

Breakfast over, we began climbing steadily, criss-crossing the terminal moraine and finally reaching a level plateau and Lobuche. Before reaching the tiny single-storeyed building which marks the settlement, my head had begun spinning. I sat on a rock and let the others pass and marvelled at the landscape, almost lunar in character, with great house-sized lumps of white rock dotting the skyline.

I got to my feet and pressed on, arriving at Lobuche to find Eric hard at work pitching the tents.

Yesterday they had had four inches of snow, but today there was no trace of it. We sat in the smoke-filled cabin nibbling digestive biscuits and sipping tea. It was difficult to breathe as the fire spluttered away with smoke billowing in all directions and with eyes reddened and streaming, I beat a hasty retreat to the relative smoke-free atmosphere of the open door.

Within a few minutes, a tall, lanky man came bouncing down the mountainside from the direction of Everest Base Camp. He had a wife and porter in tow and within a few minutes had set up surgery and was busily treating a mass of minor injuries and trivialities. He was John Mawson, a New Zealand doctor employed by the Hillary Foundation.

Since Ed Hillary climbed Everest in 1953 he has spent much time and effort, and with considerable skill and determination raised many hundreds of thousand pounds, building and establishing schools, hospitals, landing-strips and bridges for the benefit of the Sherpa community, who have over the years played such a big role in man's attempts on Everest.

John Mawson told us that he spent much of his time, when not at the base hospitals of Paphu or Khumde, touring the Sherpa villages, giving medical aid, treatment and advice. He looked extremely fit and strong, which was not surprising since he walked over 500 miles a month carrying his surgery on his back in his rucksack.

John told us that there were Americans at Everest Base Camp on a Bicentennial expedition, aiming to climb Everest by the South Col route. He'd just been up there helping out, since both of the American doctors who were with the expedition had been marooned high on the face for four days by heavy snowfall.

We asked him about weather conditions. We were worried that the monsoon was going to end prematurely but he allayed our fears. He'd heard on the American Base Camp radio that the monsoon was still in full swing and the meteorological reports indicated that it was likely to rain unabated until early October.

Mick Hopkinson did the cooking that evening. We only had one food container and that was a slimmed down version of the full box. The higher we got the more noticeable the fibre-glass in the food became. The smell nauseated me and I only managed a few mouthfuls of stew before collapsing in the relative warmth of my sleeping bag. The nights were becoming very cold and, once the sun had disappeared behind the distant ranges, it began to freeze.

Mick and I talked late into the night. I was extremely concerned about our progress. We were already running over three weeks late and, despite assurances from John Mawson, I was still extremely worried that the monsoon might end and then the river would drop rapidly, leaving us with a rock-strewn river bed that would rapidly smash our canoes. Apart from the time factor our financial position was far from healthy. Inflation in Nepal is as bad as anywhere and our own costs were escalating with the speed of the Concorde project. Would we have enough time, enough boats and enough money to do the whole length of the river? We discussed the pros, the cons and the alternatives and resolved to concentrate our efforts on the stretch of river from Base Camp to Jubing. From Jubing downwards the gradient fell off rapidly and we felt there would be far fewer problems on this lower section.

In the early hours of the morning I felt a violent urge to relieve myself and stumbled out through the flap past Mick Reynolds' and Eric Jones' tent. It was a beautiful clear night and the frost glistened on the canvas. High above, the mountains were a fascinating sight, the moon illuminating them a strange iridescent orange. An icy wind was blowing off the glacier and I quickly made my way back to the tent and the warmth of my sleeping bag, dreaming happily until dawn.

Mick Hopkinson was up early as the sun rose over the distant peaks, ready to capture the sunrise on film. I glanced at my watch. It was barely five thirty am and I curled up inside my bag, dozing fitfully until seven. Eventually Mick shook me out of my bag, and with a pounding head, I got up slowly to breakfast off porridge and John West kippers. They were delicious and, for once, there was no taste of fibre-glass.

The porters collapsed the tents whilst we ate and by nine thirty we were ready for the off. The weather had changed for the better and the sun blazed down through a brilliant blue sky. In the west, a few mackerel clouds scudded over the surrounding peaks. Both Mick Reynolds and I seemed to be suffering from the altitude and we took up the position of tailmakers until eventually at midday, with the sun reaching its high point, we reached the moraine overlooking Gorak Shep.

Mick Reynolds and I sat on the bluff overlooking the moraine. Mick Hopkinson with Eric Jones were over three-quarters of a mile away and a thousand feet below our position, for they had wandered casually off to inspect one of the many large lakes which pockmark the glaciers. It had looked very near but we sat and watched them for over an hour as they climbed back up to us, over the rubble-strewn slope with the sun relentlessly beating down. They arrived exhausted and flaked out by the side of the path, looking drained and ill. It had taken ten minutes to climb down to the lake to satisfy their curiosity but an hour to struggle back up again.

I wondered how we were going to react to the altitude once we started paddling. Was it going to be possible to paddle at that altitude with the sudden explosion of power that is required. We climbed steadily, taking frequent rests. Eric was the only one who seemed to be going well and he seemed to have tremendous powers of endurance, as he has proved by his solo mountaineering escapades, and was obviously in his element.

We arrived exhausted at Gorak Shep late that afternoon. It is a bleak, desolate place and consists of an uninhabited low-walled shelter. Everywhere are reminders of the price man has paid for his attempts on Everest and behind the shelter, carved on a cliff, was an inscription to Mick Burke, the British climber lost so tragically just below the summit on the 1975 British South-West Face expedition.

Our tents were up, and whilst our porters occupied themselves with lighting a fire, I fell into a deep, untroubled sleep.

I awoke whilst it was still dark. Eric had made some mouthwatering blackcurrant and orange Rise 'n Shine and I sipped it through cracked lips and let it trickle down a parched throat. My head was throbbing and still fully clothed, I kicked my boots off, crawled into my sleeping bag and stripped off to return to sleep.

The freezing cold in the early hours of the morning woke me again and I lay there shivering, unable to get back to sleep. At altitude, the lack of oxygen in the air makes it almost impossible, once the temperature falls below freezing point, to sleep well since body heat is rapidly lost.

At sunrise, I crawled out of the tent and walked the twenty yards or so to a small pool and stripped to the waist, washed and shaved. Personal cleanliness does tend to be a bit neglected on expeditions. I had been wearing the same shirt for four days and this was the first time I had washed for the same period!

Our porters seemed to have been awake most of the night and were huddled around the fire with shawls wrapped tightly around them. Already a half-filled kettle was simmering away, as the fire crackled slowly into life.

Pancho, in charge of our portering team, came across looking argumentative.

'Porters will not go any higher, Sahib.'

'What do you mean, Pancho,' I stormed, 'you all agreed to go up to Base Camp. We're over two-thirds of the way there and it's only another five miles.'

There followed a bitter argument with Pancho acting as

spokesman for the porters, who sat there defiantly. I knew money was at the root of the problem and all the arguments were aimed at bettering their lot. Eventually I compromised and with the promise of double wages and 'backsheesh' at the end of the trip, they agreed to the carry.

The surrounding summits were still shrouded in mist as we left for Base Camp. Within a few hundred yards we hit snow and picked our way along a badly-marked trail. The snow had a hard crust to it and crunched beneath our feet as we struggled upwards. It was totally still and eerie as we moved between towering ice-cliffs, pinnacles and soaring glacier spires. It was not until we were within a hundred yards of Base Camp that the sun finally penetrated the low cloud ceiling. There was no mistaking the splurge of colour, the bright yellow and the orange dots which marked the American Base Camp. The expedition was in full swing as we wandered into camp and a Sherpa thrust an enormous mug of tepid orange juice into our hands to quench our insatiable thirst.

I fell into conversation with Mike Hoover. He is a tall, lanky American who runs his own film company and globe-trots the world, producing and recording TV shows ranging from 'Perry Como Sings' to films such as *Eiger Sanction*, starring Clint Eastwood. He was here on Everest to produce a 200,000-dollar documentary on this American Bicentennial expedition to climb Everest by the South Col route. He was full of ideas and the original plan had been to produce live TV from the top of Everest by helicoptering a transmitter into the Western Cwm at 20,000 feet, using a satellite to shoot live coverage back to the States. In his own words he just 'couldn't get it together in time', but his claim that if he could have done it he would have had an audience second only to man landing on the moon seemed highly probable.

We learnt that the Americans had spent considerable time acclimatising on the way up, staying three days at Namche Bazar at 11,300 feet and two days at Tengpoche and yet, despite this, several of the team members had experienced altitude problems once they reached Base Camp.

Mick Reynolds began erecting his Arriflex TV camera but

no sooner did the camera appear than the Nepalese liaison officer informed us that we had no permission to film at Base Camp. He was in fact correct, not only did we not have permission to film at Base Camp but had he looked at our trekking permits he would have found they were valid only as far as Pheriche!

We saw little point in arguing, such is Nepalese officialdom, and we beat a hasty retreat, both teams wishing each other good luck, ourselves for their ascent and they for our descent.

We dropped behind a bluff and with the canoes standing vertically, framing Everest, we had our pictures taken unhindered. Mick Reynolds erected his tripod and, with us prancing around in front of the camera feeling like film stars, he shot off another cassette of movie film.

We now had to drop back down along the edge of the glacier and find a way across through the maze of ice-blocks weighing many tons, to the glacier lake where the real canoeing would begin.

It was stifling hot as we retraced our steps. The sun was burning down relentlessly and the reflection from the snow was intense. Foolishly I had forgotten snow glasses and left them at the camp site of the night before, five miles back, and it now took us three hours in the oven-like heat to drop down back to it.

We lounged around seeking shelter from the glare of the sun in the shade of the building.

Tea that night was army compo rations, a real treat with sausages, beans and tomatoes. It still looked paltry compared to the provisions the Americans had, ranging from fresh chickens, vegetables brought up every other day from Namche Bazar, to freeze-dried ice cream! Compared however to our normal fare, our meal this evening was a real feast.

We stacked the dirty plates outside the tent, fell into our sleeping bags and slept soundly until the following morning.

I awoke at six am with an intense, searing pain in my eyes. It was as though a million tiny needles were prodding my eyeballs. When I managed to open my eyelids, which were puffed up and stuck together, everything was a blur. Panic gripped me until I realised what had happened. Yesterday I had walked to Base Camp and back, much of the time without snow goggles, and was now paying the price with snow blindness. Mick Reynolds was similarly affected but in the company of Mick Hopkinson and Eric Jones he set off to scale Kala Pattar, an 18,000 footer directly opposite Everest, which looks straight into the Western Cwm and affords an unparalleled view up the sweeping flanks and avalanche-prone faces leading to the summit. For once luck was on our side and through a brilliant blue sky they succeeded in snatching some fine stills and cine film of Everest.

I spent most of the day quietly feeling sorry for myself, lying in the relative darkness of my tent. I was frightened that I might have done some permanent damage to my eyes. At midday, with the sun reaching its high point, Mick Hopkinson and Mick Reynolds together with Eric Jones reappeared. The porters were complaining vehemently. They had run out of firewood, largely because they insisted on keeping a fire burning all night, and their food stocks were now running low. There seemed nothing for it but to drop back down to Lobuche where we could purchase and barter for further stocks of firewood and food, then climb back up to the glacier lake.

I left camp as the tents were being dismantled and began the painful process of picking my way down the rock-strewn trail to Lobuche. We arrived there late in the afternoon and the porters, who had passed me on the way down, had already pitched the tents. I crawled inside, thankful to be away from the penetrating glare of the sun.

I was dosed up with painkillers but, despite that, spent a miserable night, only falling into an exhausted sleep in the early hours of the morning.

It was now September 17th. I awoke pondering the day's plan. Today we must go on to the glacier and find the glacier lake and the high point of the river, or drop back to meet up with the others. We had already been away from them for five days and if we delayed any longer we would run out of food. We might also run out of time to complete our descent before the monsoon closed. I felt extremely ill and my head, which had been clear the day before, was now pulsating madly with a splitting headache. Mick Hopkinson and Mick Reynolds felt much the same, but ignoring our discomfort we decided to go up on to the Khumbu Glacier.

Once again the porters were not enthusiastic. Pancho assumed the role of interpreter as usual, and we argued about the same problems we had discussed the previous day. With offers of double pay and more 'backsheesh' they were finally persuaded to go on to the glacier.

We ate a hurried breakfast of pancakes and stale, soggy rich tea biscuits and set out up the trail, tramping through the snow. Within two hours we reached the high point overlooking glacier lake. Here the trail ended and we had to make our way as best we could, picking our footholds through house-sized ice-blocks.

It was hard going as we scrambled and climbed across the glacier débris to reach the lake, and the relentless sun sapped our strength. At nine thirty we reached the glacier lake itself. Eric Jones placed his rucksack on the ground and pulled out an altimeter. It read 17,500 feet. Canoes had never been higher.

But would we be able to manoeuvre them in the lake to win the altitude record? We were glad to see that it was not completely iced over with a solid sheet, for we had been told that this happened under certain weather conditions. But there was not a square inch of water to be seen. As we peered at it, the lake shimmered and glinted as the sun's rays struck the moving particles of ice, all jostling into each other on the gently heaving surface: giant gleaming cubes rubbed against smaller nodules. Huge icebergs, as big as motor cars, cannoned into tiny chunks. Would our canoes get squashed between all the bumping, crunching, grinding ice? Would the larger blocks crush us against the huge bergs or would we be able to steer a dexterous course in-between?

Launching the canoes looked like being a problem. We changed rapidly into our canoeing gear and Mick Hopkinson decided the only way to get into the lake which was encircled by twenty-foot ice-walls was to seal launch. So, with cameras whirring, we strapped ourselves into the canoes, balanced on the crest of an 80° ice-slope, rocked gently backwards and forwards and, with a sudden rush, hurled simultaneously into the lake. The water was crystal clear and barely above freezing point and the minor tidal wave produced as we hit the water sent small icebergs bobbing up and down. It felt strange to be sitting in such unusual surroundings.

The ice-walls towered menacingly above us and a constant trickle of melt water ran down their sides and streamed into the lake. Mick Reynolds set up his movie camera, whilst Eric Jones was eighty feet off the deck clambering on to an ice-pinnacle to shoot some top shots. Panting in the high altitude, our bare hands gripping the wet paddles, the noses of our canoes cut narrow channels between the bobbing ice. We slid along cautiously, gently pushing the floating chunks aside, trying to avoid the icebergs and to keep a safe distance from the ice-walls.

A glacier is a river of moving ice and on the climb across the glacier we had been very conscious of its shifting movement. Occasionally we heard a crack like a rifle shot as a block of ice split away from the main mass, and a tremendous crash as it toppled into the lake, sending clouds of needle-shaped ice particles high in the air.

We paddled slowly the length of the lake. It was totally exhausting and the combination of high altitude and water, no more than 1°C, drained our strength. At one point, my canoe became trapped between two icebergs and, unable to dislodge it and fearing that the icebergs would close up and snap the canoe, I unclipped the spraysheet, climbed out and lifted the boat into a safer spot.

We pulled the two canoes alongside each other, and with the altimeter in full view of the cameras we posed, as Eric shot off half a dozen frames. It was an exciting moment to realise we had achieved a world altitude record for canoeing.

Mick Reynolds called across, 'Can you do a quick eskimo roll?'

'You must be joking! Have you felt the bloody water?' I replied.

The porters were sitting on their haunches laughing and joking as we picked our way along the lake. The sun was now high in the sky, the time was getting on. It had been a mistake to stay on the lake so late in the day, for now we were being bombarded by a constant stream of small chunks of ice and pebbles careering down runnels and becoming detached from ledges. They seemed harmless, until a whole fusillade of small rocks came rocketing down a side gully and pocked the water around the canoes. Startled and surprised, we spun around and headed away from the danger zone.

I had brought up with me from Pheriche a Bell and Howell Cassette Loading Camera. It was the type of camera originally fastened to fighter planes during the war, which was activated when the machine guns were fired so that it recorded whatever the plane shot at. We were using it for more peaceful pursuits and Leo had adapted it so that it could be used in an underwater housing bolted on to the canoe. Although not in the underwater housing, I was keen to get some shots in the ice-lake, using the 85° wide-angle lens with which the camera was fitted.

At one point the lake disappeared into an ice passage which had a roof over thirty feet up, consisting of huge ice-blocks wedged across a gap. In places this gap was no more than a boat's width. We weighed up carefully before paddling into the entrance. In the dim light, we carefully navigated our way, yard by yard, along the passage. At one point it was so narrow that the canoes could go no further, but by tipping them edge-on and pushing off the ice-wall, we found they would just slide through. It was strangely silent and still. Mick took some film of me and we decided it was time to go back. Retracing our route was infinitely more difficult, since we were unable to turn around in the three-foot gap between the walls, and laboriously had to edge our way in reverse for more than thirty feet. At last, we saw the sun glinting on the water at the entrance to the passageway. As we joined the lake there was an ominous grinding noise of ice against ice, a cascade of small ice particles and a colossal crash as an ice-block weighing over two tons came thundering down. I ducked instinctively and hunched up. We were both caught in the periphery of the ice-fall. A golf-ball sized chunk of ice hit me on the head and was deflected by my crash helmet. Mick Hopkinson's canoe was struck on the deck and a saucer-sized hole appeared. The air was full of ice particles and the canoes rocked violently as the block hit the water, no more than ten feet from us. There was no need for further warning and we sprinted away from the ice-fall. It had been a narrow escape and a few seconds earlier we would have been still in the tunnel and in the direct line of the block's descent.

With increased caution we continued around the lake, giving any unstable and unsafe looking sections of ice-cliff a wide berth. After paddling for about a quarter of a mile, our arms felt like lead and we were just about to give up when we found the place where water from the lake was seeping out through a mass of earth, ice and rocks – the source waters of the Dudh Kosi.

Manhandling the canoes out of the water, with the porters helping as our hands were numb with cold, we managed to haul them across a steep scree slope. But it was not possible to launch again, for the amount of water seeping through the jumbled débris would not have floated them. The rivulets from the melt streams of the surrounding glaciers did not look as though they joined together into a canoeable stream much above Pheriche after all.

With Eric Jones route-finding, we retraced our steps through the glacier and back on to the trail. We would be heading downhill from now on, and elated with success at capturing the world altitude record for canoeing, we dropped down to Lobuche in barely one and a half hours.

Our long session on the water had taken its toll and the Polaroid glasses, which I had been loaned by Mick Hopkinson, had done little to absorb the punishing glare from the lake. I was now extremely worried as my vision was down to a few feet and everything was a blur. However there was no time to waste resting or feeling sorry for myself, for food supplies had now run out and our porters were anxious to get back to Pheriche as quickly as possible. One of the porters took my rucksack which helped and I descended as rapidly as I could.

As I stumbled down the twisting track, I squinted at the level of water in the river to make sure that there was insufficient to float a canoe. At this height it was still a stream, although it was gaining in volume as we dropped down through the gloom which heralded the inevitable monsoon rain.

I arrived at Pheriche to find the evening meal well under way. Mick Hopkinson had purchased a bucketful of potatoes for forty pence and they were simmering away in a great aluminium pot. We ate well; new potatoes with melted butter and army compo luncheon meat, washed down with Rise 'n Shine.

That night we slept in one of the sherpa's gardens, safe from roaming yaks and scrapping dogs. I spent a cold, uncomfortable night dosed up with Codeine but in agony from my snowblindness. I was relieved when at last dawn broke.

Breakfast was Aberdeen kippers in delicious tomato sauce and then off downhill again. We wondered how Rob and the rest of the team had fared. Had they had any accidents, how many canoes would they have lost, how much of the river had they managed to do? I pondered these thoughts as I picked my way along the boulder-strewn track.

We were carrying no food with us now but buying it as we went along. We ate like lords; an omelette here, a colossal plate of rice and *dahl* there, and always *tsampa* with lashings of margarine, sweetened with coarse, irregular Nepalese sugar, mixed into a porridge with hot creamy tea. I felt myself getting stronger day by day and no longer had the pounding headache and feeling of utter exhaustion which had been the result of going up too quickly and too soon to altitude.

We covered two stages that day, dropping down from Pheriche to Namche Bazar, trying to glean information as to the whereabouts and progress of Rob's team. It had only been eight days before when we walked the same track, but

93

everything looked much greener and fresher and the whole countryside was bathed in sunshine.

At Tengpoche monastery we found a canoe broken in half and a note from Rob three days old. It was brief, saying that things were going well and giving us instructions where in Namche we would find Mick Hopkinson's trekking permit, which he needed to clear with the police before dropping further down the valley.

We made Namche by four pm that afternoon and were welcomed back at the Footrest Hotel. Mick Hoover, the film producer from the American Everest climb, was there with a hacking dry cough; he had dropped back down to try and get rid of it before making a push for the summit.

There was more *raksi*, more delicious Nepalese cooking and we sat enthralled as Eric for once came out of himself and talked late into the night about his climbing adventures. Mike Hoover's fast-talking American voice dominated the conversation for the first hour, but gradually the balance changed as he began to realise just how good Eric Jones really was and we listened spellbound as Eric recounted stories of his climbs on the Matterhorn, the Eiger, the Bonatti Pillar and the Central Pillar of Brouillard.

It was past midnight and the fire had almost died. I could stand the smoke-filled atmosphere no longer and went downstairs to get a few minutes' fresh air before turning in. It was a beautiful, star-studded night and a full moon illuminated the distant mountains. Tomorrow we would be rejoining the main party and another phase of the expedition would begin.

7

Taking to the River

WHILST MICK AND I had clambered up to Everest Base Camp and back and then paddled along the glacier lake, the main party had started down the Dudh Kosi at its earliest navigable point. This party consisted of Leo and Geoff and the five canoeists, John Gosling, John Liddell, Dave Manby, Roger Huyton and Bob Hastings. The following account of their descent from Pheriche to Phakding is compiled from the diary which they kept on a Philips cassette tape recorder. The main narrative is Roger Huyton's, with additions from John Liddell.

Within a few minutes of the Base Camp party leaving Pheriche, Santabier the chief sirdar asked for a meeting to be called between the porters and John Liddell. An old school desk was brought out into the open for John to sit at and with the porters sitting cross-legged on their haunches in a semi-circle, the meeting was convened. Santabier acted as mediator between the two sides with Pancho, the cook, emerging as the spokesman for the porters. He presented their demands. They wanted immediate advances on their wages, assurances that no more porters would be laid off, and guaranteed backsheesh and bonuses when they finished the trip.

John Liddell pointed out that the next advance was not due for a week as we had only paid them an advance the previous day. Furthermore it had all been agreed before we left Kathmandu that porters would be paid off as loads were used up. As we were paying above the going rate we could not be expected to pay any bonuses or backsheesh.

Pancho was not satisfied. He consulted the porters and resolutely represented their demands, asserting that if they were not met they would no longer work for us. It really did look as though we would have a rebellion on our hands. Whilst all this had been going on, John Gosling was listening in the background. Deciding extreme action was called for he puffed himself up until he was bright red in the face, crashed his fist down on the table and, roaring until his voice echoed around the valley, let rip.

They were no good, a lazy lot, cheating on the loads and stealing from our provisions. They were trying to ruin the expedition and if they wouldn't work, well, they were all . . . sacked! Yes, they were sacked!

There was a stunned silence and then pandemonium broke loose as everyone started shouting and arguing. The meeting disbanded in total disarray, the astonished porters retiring to one of the teahouses to consider the unprecedented action taken by 'Mr. John' as Gosling had become known to them.

An equally confused and amazed canoe team retired to their tents to discuss the implications of Gosling's action. The expedition had suddenly found itself without porters over 150 miles from Kathmandu.

Gosling reassured the others that the porters would back down and ask to be re-employed, but as the minutes ticked by even he became uneasy.

'Are you sure?' questioned John Liddell.

'Of course I am,' snapped Gosling, making furtive glances through the tent door to see if the porters were already heading back down the trail to Kathmandu. Had he taken things too far?

The meeting had been disbanded for over an hour before Santabier appeared.

'The porters have said they will continue working.'

'That's good, Santabier,' replied Liddell in his best public-school manner, 'just make sure it doesn't happen again.'

As soon as Santabier was out of earshot we all burst out laughing. Gosling's bluff had worked and we heaved a sigh of relief.

Already it was late in the morning and we had planned a full day's canoeing.

Leo began organising filming equipment whilst Rob and

Confined here within its 2,000-foot gorge, the Dudh Kosi is
impenetrable except by canoe.

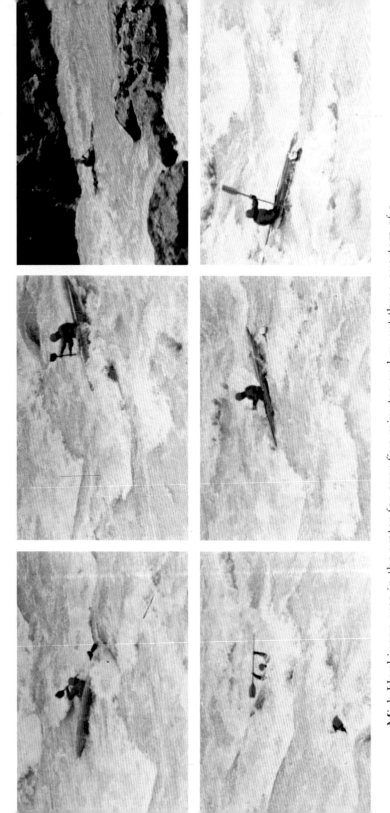

Mick Hopkinson was in the water for over five minutes and swept three-quarters of a mile before being rescued.

Dave adapted the small camera case to ensure a more rigid mounting on the canoe. The waterproof housing had been specially designed and constructed by Harry Horton from Bridgwater. A keen aqualung diver, he had become disillusioned with trying to obtain inexpensive but high quality waterproof housings to enable him to follow his second hobby of underwater photography. He started making housings for his own cameras, made a few for friends and before long found he had a full-scale business on his hands, which grew rapidly and he now exports to most corners of the world. Our request for a canoe-mounted camera housing was somewhat out of the ordinary, but he entered into the spirit of things and designed and built a fine, lightweight casing that housed a Bell and Howell Cassette camera which had been converted from clockwork to a motor drive by one of Leo's electronics friends.

The only problem with the set-up was that the single bolt mounting on the canoe was not rigid enough to hold the camera steady and it was necessary to wind long strips of tape around the camera and boat to ensure a solid mounting. The film shot on the camera was incredible and gave viewers at first hand the same view of the rapids the canoeist has as he paddles along.

When we arrived the previous day, the cloud base was low which gave us little impression of the true grandeur of our surroundings. As work progressed the cloud lifted and we found we were encircled by dramatic snow-covered peaks, towering above us, the sun defining each ridge, crest and gully to perfect sharpness, the shadows and snow contrasted against the deep blue sky.

Meanwhile Gosling was haranguing the porters. He wasn't going to let them forget their earlier misdemeanours as he organised loads for them to carry back downhill to the evening's camp site. They found it difficult to understand why after carrying twelve canoes to 14,000 feet up the Himalayas for seventeen days, across all the major river valleys on the Everest trek, they were not all being used but that they were now being asked to turn round and carry some of them back down again. It was beyond their comprehension. John was enjoying every minute of it, bullying and cajoling the porters as he saw each of them off downhill.

At last everything was ready and we walked down towards the river which snakes an erratic shallow course over rocks and boulders. With Roger Huyton, John Liddell and John Gosling in support on the bank, Rob and Dave entered the water. They made slow progress in the shallow, rocky water with cascading falls and chutes only just wide enough to steer the canoes through. The water was unrelenting. To wedge the canoe broadside on to the current would have been disastrous, with little chance of releasing it before the pressure of the water snapped it in half like a matchstick.

Despite their double seams and Kevlar reinforcing at the most vulnerable points, the canoes were taking a severe battering from partly submerged rocks, and already cracks were beginning to appear in their hulls.

After the first three-quarters of a mile Rob pulled into the side. The water was so shallow in places he was having difficulty using his paddle to steer and as he had tried to make a stroke, the paddle would be ripped out of his hand as the blade struck a boulder or jammed between two rocks.

Dave pulled in beside Rob and they rested in the eddy, chests heaving as they took in deep breaths to oxygen-starved lungs. Canoeing at this sort of altitude, where the air is thinned of its oxygen, in ice-cold waters, is demanding and rapidly saps the strength. Although they had been on the water for no more than fifteen minutes, they both felt drained.

Whilst the camera team worked their way downstream, Dave and Rob rested until a signal from Leo indicated that all was ready. Pushing off, the two canoeists were carried downstream, dodging rocks and weaving their way along the continuous rapids, stopping every few minutes by the bank to rest up and take stock of their position.

In two hours they had covered three miles and found the river becoming wider and deeper. In places it was over forty feet wide, which contrasted with the narrow twenty-feet torrent they had started off on at Pheriche. The river varied enormously in depth but could be as much as ten or twelve feet deep in patches in the main channel. The bed was irregular and boulder strewn so that it was necessary for the canoeists to twist and turn their craft from bank to bank in order to avoid being capsized.

A canoeist sits in his craft with his legs stuck straight out in front of him at right angles, his head is only just above the water level and his face is constantly covered in spray. His angle of vision is very low, yet he must try to see what lies ahead as he hurtles down at over thirty miles an hour, interpret the best channel to take and estimate how steep a rapid is, how much water there will be in the shallower parts, where he can 'break-out' of a counter current or where he can slide into the bank for a breather. All this requires split-second judgment and timing which is most exhausting at high altitude for the lack of oxygen slows thinking speed right down. He cannot see over giant boulders but must swing round them with his paddle whirling, hoping nothing alarming lies beyond. All the time he is being swept along he must try to maintain his balance, keep the canoe upright, try to keep it going forwards and not get twisted round in eddies so that he is facing backwards and cannot see what lies ahead. Even one eskimo roll in rough water here would be exhausting because it was hard enough to get air into our lungs when right side up, but to be submerged for several minutes in such icy water, unable to breathe, would be excruciatingly painful. Two eskimo rolls in quick succession would clearly be dangerous. Above all, the canoeist in such a boulder-strewn river would have to try not to turn turtle and so be dragged along the bottom on his head. The art of canoeing lies in 'reading' the water in such a way that the canoe can be steered in balance into the smoothest water along the line of least resistance by instantaneous decisions. Ninety per cent of the job is planning the route, and John Gosling was playing a vital role, surveying the hazards ahead from the river bank.

The Dudh Kosi presented a myriad of problems in quick succession: stoppers, haystacks, rapids, cataracts, standing waves, steep, narrow gorges and boulders, boulders, boulders all the way. The icy water soused over us the entire time, so that we could hardly see or breathe. It was like being a piece of flotsam in a tumble dryer.

There just didn't seem to be any smooth water at all. It was chute after chute with another rip of white water at the end of each. To break-out of a stopper it is often necessary to paddle along it to where the water breaks. In most rivers there would then be a stretch of calm before the next stopper, but here the canoeist would paddle along the stopper to the break flow towards one bank, only to find that the water then twisted back on itself in a foaming wave; through that and then a series of eddies behind ragged boulders which seemed to block the whole river. Sometimes the channel between the rocks was so narrow the canoe would be buffeted from side to side; as it was released from the straitjacket it would be whipped round to face the wrong way.

As the day wore on, however, Dave and Rob began to gain confidence and became more used to the speed of the water, shooting the river in short stretches and alternating the lead as they worked their way slowly downstream. Because their faces and hands were permanently wet with icy water, and because their arms felt like lead from exercising so hard at such a high altitude and because they were so short of oxygen, they had to pull into the bank frequently, whenever they could find a suitable spot. Unfortunately these calmer backwater patches near the bank were few and far between. They were often so far apart that the canoeists were forced to continue in explosive action a great deal longer than they wanted to. Once stopped, they just sat in their canoes, chests heaving, water dripping from their faces, gasping for breath. One of the shore party would hold the canoes steady for them as they panted away, and John Gosling would come racing up with information of what lay ahead.

John Gosling was on the bank doing a magnificent job, surveying and checking out the rapids in front of the canoe team and racing back upstream to shout out instructions to Rob and Dave. To the right of this rock, to the left of another, watch out for the overhanging tree or a stopper, each of his instructions was carefully memorised.

Suddenly they were in trouble. Dave capsized and his upturned canoe was rapidly swept downstream. He missed his first roll and we watched as his paddle appeared for a second attempt. As it was a shallow rocky stretch of water with little more than three feet at the deepest point Dave's head repeatedly struck submerged rocks and only his crash helmet saved him from serious injury. His paddle caught on a rock and was almost wrenched from his grasp and, with lungs near to bursting point, he abandoned the canoe and started swimming.

John Gosling raced along the right bank, trying to keep up with Dave as he was swept rapidly downstream. Leaping from boulder to boulder, at times landing short and awkwardly, Gosling searched anxiously for a place where the river narrowed, where he could reach Dave. Rob too had beached his canoe and was on the opposite bank, trying to catch up with Dave who was rapidly outpacing his rescuers.

Dave was in grave trouble. Too shallow to swim and too deep to keep a sure footing, he was crashing and colliding with rocks, and being up-ended and rolled over and over by the current.

Suddenly a ray of hope, as Dave was caught in an eddy and Rob Hastings, oblivious of his own safety, leapt into the racing water and waded into the main current. As he reached out with outstretched hands, Dave, who was no more than a foot away, was plucked out of his grasp and continued downstream.

From the bank, we could see Dave was fighting for his life. We watched as he was swept over drops and churned around in stoppers and carried past backwaters and eddies. He seemed past caring. Battered and bruised with waves crashing all around, he had given up trying to swim and was concentrating on getting a breath before inevitably he was submerged again.

But luck was on Dave's side. Over a hundred yards downstream from his capsize, he was caught in an eddy and this time Rob managed to grasp Dave's lifejacket and haul him on to the bank. He was shivering violently, blanched white with the cold and his lips were blue from the lack of oxygen. Leo arrived and produced a dry sweater which Rob helped Dave into. He was unable to talk and wheezed and spluttered as he gasped in lungfuls of air. He was shocked and battered and every inch of his body was badly bruised and scarred from being swept over rocks. It took him over twenty minutes to recover and, easing sore and aching limbs into protesting movement, he was helped to the camp site.

Only when we walked on downstream did we realise how lucky Dave had been, since the river steepened considerably and no one would have survived swimming through the massive waterfalls and rock chokes.

Meanwhile John Gosling and Rob Hastings had located the canoe. As a precaution, all the canoes had been packed full of buoyancy and this probably saved it from being broken up. It was trapped against a large rock in the river. Wading across the shallows, Rob recovered it, hoping that we would be able to patch it but the seams were split completely down both sides, and a huge hole had been torn out of the deck. It was a write off and was given to the porters, and later left at Tengpoche monastery where it is now a chicken house of unique design.

Our first day on the river had been an eye-opener. Everyone had been taken by surprise at the speed of the water and degree of difficulty of the rapids. Dave was still badly shocked by his swim and we had suddenly become aware of how dangerous the river could be. We turned in early, wondering what further surprises the river had in store for us.

The following morning, a heavy mist was swirling in the Dudh Kosi valley and we delayed our start. The mist suddenly rolled away revealing Nuptse, Lhotse and Everest standing magnificently at the head of the valley.

With Everest clearly visible, the team launched their boats. John Liddell joined Rob and Roger on the water. He was feeling very weak, and only just beginning to recover from a serious bout of dysentery which he had picked up on the walk in. No sooner had he clipped the spraysheet on to the cockpit, than he was caught by the current and swept out of the eddy. Taken completely by surprise at the speed of the water, he disappeared backwards out of control over the lip of a fall and into a series of enormous breaking waves and stoppers. Miraculously he appeared unscathed at the bottom and waited in an eddy for the others to drop down.

Rob Hastings was in fine form, confidently leading the team through a mile-stretch of highly demanding and testing rapids, dodging between rocks to avoid the worst of the water hazards.

And then Rob found himself in difficulties. Momentarily he lost control of the canoe and the bow swung round and caught on a partly submerged rock. Within seconds he was broadside on to the current and the pressure of water on the deck capsized the canoe, wedging it against the rock. He felt the whole canoe splintering and then slowly parting company with the rock. He rolled up and headed for the bank, realising he had a few seconds in which to make it before the badly damaged canoe sank, and he was left swimming in the centre of the river. John Gosling caught the boat as it closed in and dragged it ashore. It had split completely across the back deck and was a write off. Had it not broken, there is little doubt Rob would have been pinned in the canoe against the rock with small chance of rescue in those swirling waters.

Cold, wet and tired the team adjourned for lunch. A replacement boat was called for and, whilst we waited for this, we stripped off and warmed up in the afternoon sun.

John Liddell looked ill and was slumped down by the canoes. Dysentery is debilitating at the best of times and during the morning he had been stopping frequently to relieve himself. Determined to pull his weight on the expedition, he had forced himself to canoe but now felt unable to carry on. Dave Manby who had recovered from his battering of the day before took over.

The afternoon went slowly and it was past three by the time we arrived at Pangpoche bridge above Tengpoche monastery. The whole width of the river was compressed into a narrow chasm, twenty feet deep and no more than three feet wide, with the water churning its way through. It would be suicidal to try canoeing through that and we decided to shoot the rapids to a point twenty yards above the bridge. Each foot of the lead-up rapid was carefully scrutinised and break-out points noted. It was vitally important to make sure the canoes stopped in good time before the fall, and catchers were positioned on the bank to try to stop the canoeists, should they miss their break-outs.

Rob led through, coming down with the TV camera strapped to his canoe. There were only two possible break-outs and he missed the first by a foot and only just made the second.

Roger Huyton was not so lucky. He capsized in no more than one foot of water and, with his helmet scraping along the river bed, was forced to abandon his canoe.

He was five feet away from the bank and struck out against the current, managing to snatch hold of a rock and drag himself on to the bank. His canoe was swept downstream, disappeared beneath the bridge and jammed irretrievably in the narrow gap.

Camera gear was dismantled, canoes dried and stacked and the team adjourned to a *chang* house to talk and drink until supper was ready.

An Englishman appeared in the doorway. Tall, lean and athletic, he had just come down from Everest Base Camp.

'Hey, you guys aren't anything to do with those madmen up on the glacier?'

'Madmen?' enquired John Liddell.

'Yes, madmen! There's some guys up there at 18,000 feet wandering across the glacier with canoes.'

Liddell reassured our visitor, concluding his remarks with, 'They can't possibly be mad, one of them's a doctor.'

Our friend wasn't convinced and raced off towards Namche. At least we knew Mick Hopkinson and Mike Jones were now up on the glacier.

Friday, September 17th.

Once again Rob was the mainstay of the party, route finding, leading down the rapids and making the inevitable decision to portage round waterfalls and rock chokes where there was no way through. It was a disappointing day with many impossible sections, where Rob reluctantly had to call a halt to the canoeing and haul the boats from the water. It was difficult, tiring work and we made little progress.

104

Disillusioned, we left the river and climbed to Tengpoche monastery.

As we walked uphill an old wizened man, speaking in English, introduced himself to us and invited the expedition into his small smoke-filled house and promptly produced an enormous urn of *chang*. Within a few minutes everyone was sitting around with half-pint glasses of *chang* listening to Dawa. He was a fascinating character, having worked as a sherpa on the early Everest Reconnaissance expeditions led by Hugh Ruttledge in 1933 and Eric Shipton in 1935. He had also been a member of the first successful Everest expedition led by John Hunt in 1953. Mementos and old, faded photographs were passed around. He had watched our antics on the river and assured us that climbing Everest was safer than canoeing the Dudh Kosi.

Befuddled with *chang*, we thanked our host and wandered up to the monastery and to our tents pitched in a small meadow.

Below Tengpoche the river disappeared into a narrow, steep-sided, inaccessible gorge and the following morning climbing ropes were uncoiled, harnesses checked out and pitons and karabiners collected together for Rob and Leo to climb into the gorge through dense vegetation and inspect the river. Rob, wearing his canoeing gear with a canoe standing by to lower down the two hundred feet rock face, clipped on to the rope, cautiously climbed over the edge and began his abseil. Leo set up his camera and on the subsequent film record John Gosling is shown expertly paying out rope as Rob descends. Had Rob known that Gosling had never seen a climbing rope before and had picked his technique up from a picture he had seen in a Chris Bonington climbing book, perhaps he would have had second thoughts about being held by Gosling two hundred feet above the deck.

Rob inspected the gorge for several minutes before reaching a decision. With one hundred-foot waterfalls and massive rock chokes, it was beyond our capabilities. Reluctantly he decided to portage the entire gorge section. He clipped on to the rope and began prussiking back up the fixed rope and, unfamiliar with the clamps he was using, got in an awful tangle, eventually arriving red-faced and exhausted at Gosling's stance. The ropes were coiled up and the canoes packed for the carry to Namche, where we would once again take to the river.

We wound our way along the trail above the gorge. It was a bleak inhospitable place with chock stones the size of houses wedged across the gorge, forming a natural bridge fifty feet above the river. We stopped at Namche overnight and dropped down to the confluence of the Dudh Kosi and Bhote Kosi early the next morning. There were still long cold shadows in the valley and we waited for the sun to come up.

The canoes were taking a tremendous pounding and Rob Hastings, practical as ever, checked over each hull, repairing cracks and holes with plastic tape. We had a comprehensive fibre-glass repair kit but found that tape, if applied with the canoe perfectly dry, did an adequate job as well as being rapid and easy to apply.

The paddles too were taking a hammering and Rob closely inspected the shaft and blades of our wooden Prijons and Lendals. To break a paddle on the Dudh Kosi would be as disastrous to a canoeist as a climber losing his ice axe on the summit of Everest.

Other items of equipment were beginning to show signs of wear. Several of the neoprene spraysheets had developed holes and tears and we had all taken to wearing two of them at once to keep the canoe watertight.

Whilst Rob worked, John Liddell checked out the river. Gradually the gradient was lessening and the river was becoming deeper, wider and more like the water we had trained on in Austria and Switzerland, but ahead lay a big fall. It is possible to shoot a ten-foot vertical drop but anything much bigger may prove fatal. It is rare however to find such a fall stretching right across a river. Usually there is a sloping section somewhere along the fall's length where it is possible to shoot through. John went along to check this one out. It was an enormous grade-six fall under the bridge spanning the Dudh and Bhote Kosi with a series of haystacks and stoppers. Leo positioned himself below the rapids to wait for the excitement, whilst John, Rob Hastings and Dave Manby launched upstream.

Leo was probably as astonished and amazed as everyone else when first Rob, then Dave and finally John all appeared and shot through the fall, one after the other, and all going backwards!

'I know you guys are canoe slalomists and as used to going backwards as you are forwards down rapids, but when I saw you all coming backwards down the fall I thought you'd all flipped,' Leo remarked afterwards.

In reality all three canoeists had been caught in an enormous whirlpool above the fall and each in turn had been spat out, going backwards and had been unable to turn around before being swept down the fall.

A solitary break-out thirty yards downstream provided the only refuge and all three paddlers made for it with varying degrees of style and success.

The river was a worthy and unrelenting adversary, the slightest lack of skill or concentration was inviting savage punishment. The all-powerful, thrusting, brooding and above all, capricious goddess of the Dudh Kosi was not a lady to be trifled with; she never ceased to surprise. Once again the paddlers had bruised bodies and damaged boats to prove the contemptuous power of the river, once again their luck had held.

Then from the canoeing to the porters and their problems; John Liddell was involved in another exhausting two-hour negotiation with them. 'They never give up!' said John, but eventually they did.

Next morning we consolidated our position on the river. The camp site was shifted down to Phakding, from where we could work upstream and downstream on the river and make more permanent repairs to the canoes.

In the afternoon we spent three hours on the river shooting a short section of rapids from our previous day's high-point to a position two miles above the camp site. It was an uneventful, pleasant day and we felt that at last we were coming to grips with the river as we turned in that night, feeling optimistic of success.

8

Man Overboard

MIKE JONES TAKES UP the story. Mick Hopkinson, Mick Reynolds, Eric Jones and I left Namche at six thirty am. We had achieved our altitude record and were now threading our way through the early-morning mist down the steep hill beside the Dudh Kosi. The river was still in high flood, racing and pounding over partly submerged rocks. We wondered how the others had fared. If anything, it looked more difficult than when we had seen it on the way up, since there were now many more rocks showing themselves menacingly above water level.

The others raced ahead leaving me still half-blind to pick my way along the trail by the side of the river. I stopped for tea at a small hamlet by the side of a tumbling mountain stream and sat alone absorbing the sights, smells and sounds of the Nepalese countryside. I pushed on and struggled into camp at Phakding by nine am to be greeted enthusiastically by the rest of the team. Leo had a battery of cameras at the ready, and John Gosling was busy conjuring up breakfast for the new arrivals. Someone produced a mirror and I looked in disbelief at the hazy image which passed for my face: with cracked and bleeding lips and puffy bloodshot eyes, it looked more like the face of a heavyweight boxer.

We had been separated for over a week and had many tales of adventures to swop. We heard about Dave's almost tragic swim, Roger's narrow escape at Pangpoche bridge and John Gosling's saving of Rob when his boat was broken in half. It felt good to be back again and I sat on the low stone wall facing the teahouse, drinking tea and talking to John Liddell who was recounting the problems he was having with the porters. A gaggle of children were looking on eagerly, awaiting the inevitable excitement on the river.

I noticed the boats in a corner of the camp site and walked over to inspect them. The rough water had taken a heavy toll on the canoes and we were now down to eight boats, both Rob and Dave having written some off. Of those remaining, several had taken a severe battering on the river and were in need of repair. We had lost six canoes in Austria at the beginning of our trip and this white water was much more hazardous, so we were really not doing too badly provided we had enough craft left to accomplish the whole journey to the end. I had planned for considerable canoe wastage and was, so far, within my estimated limits, though I did wonder whether I ought to send down to Jubing and have the two spare craft stored there brought up to our present position.

But there were more important problems to sort out. We had made a catastrophic mistake calculating the amount of money we had brought with us and, with the nearest banks in Kathmandu, were fast running out of money to pay the porters' wages. John Liddell had foreseen the situation arising over the last week and three days ago had sent John Gosling to the air-strip at Luglha with a letter to be sent out on the first plane, requesting Mike Cheney to debit the expedition with £1,000 and send this out in small de-nomination bills so that porters could be paid off. Assess-ing the situation, it seemed unlikely that any planes would be landing at Luglha in the next two weeks, as the landing field could well have been flooded by the heavy monsoon rain we were still having. The only alternative was to send a runner out to Kathmandu to collect the money and run back in again, and we decided that this was the only way we could sort out an almost impossible situation.

A lanky youth volunteered for the job. He swore that he knew the route for the hundred miles back to Kathmandu and that he would do it there and back again at full speed. It was a long, tough journey even with any short cuts he might know about, much of it across rugged, mountainous country. The odd runner had passed us on our walk out, so we knew that they did not actually run all the way but rather kept up a much faster than average walking speed. They were nimble movers with strong ankles, able to descend the steep hills with agility and to lope up the other side without pausing. Sometimes they could be seen jumping from tussock to tussock on the more uneven ground, and they seldom stumbled.

There was still canoeing to be done. We had reached a point approximately four miles above the camp site at Phakding and by ten am were ready to walk back upstream and start canoeing. The boats were already on their way and Leo was rushing around trying to organise porters to carry his camera gear up. At the last minute, when he was ready to set off, his men decided it was teabreak and sat down and began to brew a pot of tea. At this point Leo flew into a violent rage, spitting and stamping around the camp site like a mad bull. Nothing would hurry the porters and in their own time they drank their tea and finally agreed to the carry.

I was feeling physically and mentally drained, and my eyesight was still hazy and blurred but felt I ought to make the effort and get on the water. It was a hot walk back upstream and I sauntered alongside Roger Huyton. He told me that if it had not been for Rob, very little canoeing would have been done as both he and John Liddell had been ill for several days with violent bouts of dysentery, and Dave, after his epic swim, had also been unwell.

We arrived to find the canoes sitting beside a formidable rapid. Mick Hopkinson and Rob were to shoot the fall and I settled down at the foot of the rapid to record on film the pair coming through.

It was a rugged section with the whole volume of the Dudh Kosi compressed into a gap no more than ten feet wide between two large rock masses. It would be a difficult shoot with two consecutive stoppers at the top, dropping twenty feet into a further stopper.

Mick appeared first. Despite his long lay off he looked quick and precise as he negotiated the stoppers above the fall. He was almost pushed too far over but with a quick heave on his paddle managed to manoeuvre the boat down the centre of the shoot. A quick support stroke as he hit the stopper and was momentarily held by it and then he powered the canoe into an eddy on the right-hand bank. He made it all look very easy.

Rob Hastings wasn't quite so lucky. He got thrown by the stopper at the top of the fall just as Mick had done and desperately stroking on the right to try to get a line down the shoot, he suddenly went over. I dropped the camera and watched horrified as he was swept towards the rocks. Amazingly he managed to roll first time but was now travelling backwards and within a few seconds was swept against a large rock and capsized again. I wondered whether he would manage to roll a second time as he was swept downstream. With a perfectly executed roll he reappeared and, looking very cool, made the same break-out that Mick was sitting in. It had been a fine descent and two excellent recoveries by Rob.

Now it was my turn. I handed over the camera and walked slowly back upstream to my waiting canoe, which I carefully lowered into the boiling water. It was difficult to get into the canoe as the water was like a bubbling cauldron, rising and falling every few seconds. Finally, with a porter holding the canoe, I managed to climb in and wedge myself tightly into the cockpit. I went through the routine of checking that my spraysheet was clipped securely around the cockpit, lifejacket tapes tied, adjusted my safety helmet and with cupped hands splashed water over my face. No matter how often you shoot grade six rapids the adrenalin always starts pumping around just before the off.

I pointed the bow out into the current and headed for the break-out on the opposite bank where Mick and Rob were recovering. Once again the speed was deceptive and as I pointed the bow out it was caught by the current and swept around. A wave crashed over my head and immediately gave me a splitting headache; it was ice cold and by the time I reached the eddy my hands were numb. I sat the boat behind a rock and, bobbing up and down, blew into my cupped hands to try to get the circulation back into frozen fingers.

John Liddell was trying to launch his canoe. I noticed in camp that he was looking increasingly ill and now he was having big problems even getting the canoe to the water's edge. Eventually Santabier noticed his difficulties, clambered down the bank and helped him in. John had lost a tremendous amount of weight, and was very weak as he began his ferry glide to my position but was immediately swept around and carried off downstream. He was heading for some very big, evil-looking stoppers and seemed to have little strength to steer the canoe out of trouble. John Gosling had reacted instantaneously and was racing alongside on the bank and, with no time to spare, he leapt down and grasped the bow loop of Liddell's boat before he was swept over the fall. John looked pale and drawn as he climbed out of the canoe and retired to watch. He was desperately disappointed.

Unaware of the drama, Mick Hopkinson and Rob Hastings had pushed on and were now over a hundred yards downstream, sitting in an eddy below a bridge crowded with laughing and jostling spectators.

I set off again, steadying the canoe as I hit the main stream of the rapids. Waves, stoppers, haystacks, at times blinded by the spray, it required intense concentration to pick a route through the numerous water and rock hazards. I felt shaky and my eyesight was far from perfect and whilst I could see clearly for two boat lengths in front, any greater distance than this and things appeared hazy and blurred.

I was within twenty yards of Mick and Rob's break-out when I hit an enormous five-foot-high stopper wave lining the whole width of the river and probably twenty feet long.

I braced on the wall of white water as the canoe was trapped broadside on. Normally a stopper 'runs' one way or another, that is to say, although at right angles to the direction of flow of the river, the water has a tendency to run towards the left or the right. The only exit appeared to be on the right-hand side and, bucketing up and down, I fought my way along the wall of white water and after what seemed a lifetime but was no more than a minute, crawled out of the end. I sat in the eddy and tried to recover sufficiently to ferry glide across to Mick and Rob.

Rob had experienced an even more hair-raising descent. He described what happened on the tape diary that evening: 'From the second the canoe hit the stopper I was

Our activities on and off the water provided non-stop family entertainment for the people of the Dudh Kosi valley.

The Dudh Kosi empties its swirling, milky waters into the grey Sun Kosi. Shingle banks mark the end of the monsoon.

completely lost and all I remember was continually rolling and rolling and not knowing what was happening and eventually on the fourth or fifth roll being swept clear of it.'

Leo was filming alongside the stopper and estimated that Rob had been trapped in the swirling backlash for over two minutes.

Stoppers are terrifying unless one is used to them. To escape requires a cool nerve, fine sense of balance and rapid assessment of the best route out since sitting in a stopper for any length of time requires the expenditure of a tremendous amount of energy. You have to paddle against the water power and exert enormous force whilst being shaken up and down.

If the canoe hits the stopper head on, as long as it is no more than two feet high, the momentum will carry it through. Anything more than this and the canoe is stopped dead, the back wave presses on the stern, which tips up and the canoe 'loops' vertically in the air, more often than not falling back and becoming trapped broadside on to the flow of the river in the stopper wave.

We left the camera team and headed off downstream, the swirling waters carrying us along at over thirty miles per hour. The locals chased us along the bank, the children laughing and shouting as we diced our way down some hairy white water.

At midday we arrived at the biggest fall we had seen on the river so far. We pulled out on the right-hand bank and carefully inspected the drop. It was over fifteen feet high, angled at 80°, dropping straight down into a massive stopper. We stood watching the water as it thundered and churned. To be caught in the stoppper would be fatal since two large granite rocks blocked the exits. On the walk up we had cast cursory glances at the fall. From fifty feet up it had looked minuscule but now down at water level it was a formidable problem. Mick Hopkinson sized it up and I sat watching as he prepared himself for the shoot. He decided to shoot it in the centre where there was a small rock, which caused a run through in the stopper. We watched with bated breath as he lined up and headed for the rock and then, almost in slow motion, hit the lip of the fall. The canoe tilted and accelerated down the almost vertical drop into the stopper, shuddered to a stop as it was caught and, with Mick bracing hard, travelled the length of the stopper and reappeared on the left side of the river. It had been a fine shoot and we all heaved a sigh of relief.

I took a back seat as we carried on downstream, Mick and Rob alternating the lead between them. Leading is very demanding, requiring considerable experience and skill, and a steady nerve. A climber can stand at the foot of a seemingly impossible vertical slab of rock and, using the experience he has built up over the years, spot the lines of weakness which will enable the face to be scaled. Similarly, a canoeist can look at a rapid and decide on a line down it, avoiding the worst of the rock and water hazards. The only difference is that the climber has all the time in the world to choose a route, whereas more often than not the only way a line can be spotted on the water is when the canoe is under way, which leaves the canoeist only a few seconds.

Mick Hopkinson is an excellent judge of what will go and what will not, and the best line of weakness down a rapid, despite the fact he is almost blind without his glasses. He is never one to waste time and if he thinks a rapid will go, has enough confidence in his ability to take the lead. Leading puts you completely out on your own, because he who goes first has no one to rescue him at the bottom of the rapid, should he get into difficulties.

Of course picking a line on the move does occasionally come unstuck and both Mick and I remember an occasion on the Blue Nile in Africa, when we made an almost fatal mistake reading the river from the water and Mick paddled straight over the top of a twenty-foot waterfall which I had thought to be a two-foot drop!

By two that afternoon, we had covered barely four miles from our starting point. Fall followed fall, there was no let up and no respite from the continuous rapids. Leo was on the bank and we paddled across to him and sat resting in a sheltered eddy. Pancho appeared with a giant thermos of soup and some squashed Mars Bars. The soup was wonderfully warming and I sipped it through cupped hands, trying to get the feeling back into my numbed and blanched fingers.

I instantly recognised the smell of fibre-glass on the Mars Bar and threw it to one of the gawping kids standing watching. We had been on the go for over six hours and were all feeling completely tired.

Leo intended filming us together as we shot the next rapid and his filming gear was perched high on the rocks above. It was a long rapid and, looking downstream, there were over a hundred yards of continuous white water with stopper following stopper and some formidable haystacks. The river then turned at right angles and disappeared in a sweeping right-angled bend. It looked a dicey section and I half-wondered whether we ought to leave it until the next day, when suddenly a tremendous commotion broke out as someone yelled:

'Mick, he's in the water swimming.'

I jerked round and saw Mick's orange lifejacket barely keeping him afloat as he frantically stroked for the bank. There was no sign of his canoe and paddles. I was amazed. Mick was by himself and yet where was Rob? I looked back and saw Rob sitting on a rock and out of his canoe. I yelled out to Roger to hold my canoe as I scrambled aboard. Mick was travelling slowly, his arms flailing madly. Once out of your canoe, it is difficult to swim since waves continually break over your head and stoppers submerge you.

To rescue a swimmer from a major rapid requires precise boat control. There is no opportunity to pick your line down a rapid and you must go wherever the swimmer is.

I powered across the current to where Mick was floundering and as I crossed caught sight of red fibre-glass, the deck of the totally submerged canoe as it was swept along. Within a few seconds I was up with Mick. He looked totally exhausted and I spun the canoe around so that he could take hold of the stern rope. He had hold with one hand as we dropped into an enormous stopper. There was a crash on the hull of the canoe, whether it was Mick's head or the canoe striking the rock I wasn't sure, and I looked desperately round trying to find him as he had lost contact with the stern rope. He was ten yards to my left and had given up swimming, and was being swept along in the main stream of the current, much of the time submerged by the weight of water. I lost him again and by now was getting into difficulties myself, as we were pushed to the right of centre and each stopper was becoming harder and harder to break through.

Mick was receiving a tremendous buffeting as he was swept over rocks and up-ended in stopper waves. He was making a few feeble strokes but was utterly exhausted and I knew there was very little time to get him out, since in water at that altitude and temperature survival can be measured in minutes.

Now in a very precarious position, being swept into a large rock against which the whole force of the current was directed, we were both heading rapidly towards a seemingly impossible situation. To be trapped against the rock, pinned there by the current, would offer little hope of survival. Frantically I searched for an escape route out and with a fraction of a second to spare, realised there was a small shoot, no more than four feet wide, to the right of the rock. Summoning my last reserves of energy, I back-paddled, slewing the canoe around and, with no more than one inch to spare, dropped through the shoot.

The canoe broke out behind the rock and I gasped for breath through a parched throat. In those few seconds I imagined Mick was trapped by the rock beneath the water and then miraculously he reappeared. Gathering my last ounce of strength, I shot across the current.

He was almost unconscious.

'Swim, you silly bugger, swim!' I yelled out, but above the roar of the water everything seemed drowned.

We were now into a small canyon and I was becoming extremely worried, since from the reconnaissance on the walk up I knew there was a large waterfall which could be no more than 200 yards from our present position. Mick had managed to grasp the stern loop of the canoe and I was hastily trying to steer across to the right-hand bank, but with twelve stone deadweight on the back it was an almost impossible task.

The fall was imminent. There was no more than twenty yards to the lip of the fifteen-foot drop and I knew there was one more chance and with a final effort, levered hard on the left-hand side. To my surprise the canoe responded and began to break out.

'Swim, it's your last chance,' I shouted but Mick was past caring and just hung on.

Rocking madly into the eddy and dropping my paddle in the shallow water, frantically I grasped at the branch of a tree as the canoe crunched into the rocks lining the bank. Mick released his hold on the canoe and, shocked and confused, crawled half out of the water before collapsing. Fortunately four porters were at hand and dived through the undergrowth to drag him out of the water.

Meanwhile I had been unable to hold on to the bank any longer and had been swept downstream, coming to rest no more than a boat length above the waterfall. I beached the canoe and scrambled through the dense undergrowth to where a crowd of porters were gathered around Mick. He looked deathly white but was breathing in short, bubbling gasps as we stripped off his freezing clothes and replaced them with warm ones. He was confused and covered in lacerations and bruises where he had been swept over and against the many rocks in the river bed. Dave came dashing down the trail and a distraught Rob came scrambling up from the river. Mick was safe, but what a battering he had gone through! The relief felt throughout the party was immense for he had been in great danger.

Making sure he was well looked after and still in one piece, we left Mick to the care of Dave Manby and the porters. Rob and I climbed down to the river. We pushed on taking as few risks as possible, following the safest line down rapids to avoid a repetition of Mick's near disastrous swim.

Even taking the safest route, at one point my canoe became wedged almost vertical on a small, rocky waterfall. Only prompt action by Rob, who leapt out and pulled the jammed canoe off, saved it snapping in half.

We arrived at Phakding by three pm. Mick was the centre of attention and he was still looking badly shaken by his experience. He was very lucky to be alive.

We changed and sat on a large flat rock by the side of the river, drinking tea and absorbing some warmth from the sun. The flies abounded, attracted by the stench of rotting food and human excreta deposited behind the teahouse.

We were all deeply shocked by the accident. It brought back Chris Bonington's warnings of the danger of tackling the Dudh Kosi. In over ten years of canoeing, I had never seen anyone cheat death as Mick had done, surviving a long and difficult swim in such extreme temperature and altitude conditions. We estimated he had been in the water for over five minutes and covered three-quarters of a mile.

Across at the teahouse a commotion broke out. Santabier came over and informed us that one of the porters had spotted Mick's boat upstream, trapped against a rock. Despite being on the water all day Rob volunteered to go back upstream with Leo to investigate.

Ten minutes upstream they found the canoe trapped broadside on to the current and over ten feet out from the bank. With so many canoes damaged and written off, it seemed essential to recover it and use it as a reserve boat. Rob was running out of dry clothes by now so he stripped off and, wearing no more than a pair of shorts and a light-weight anorak, took a line from Leo and, going upstream of the canoe, prepared to launch himself across the current. It was icy cold as he plunged into the racing torrent and struck out towards the canoe. At one point it looked as though he would miss it, but with two well-timed strokes he caught hold of the stern deck loop. The water had wedged the canoe, making it difficult to dislodge but with a tremendous wrench Rob heaved it off. Tied to the line, Rob and canoe were brought into the bank and hauled out. The canoe was split in two down the seams but a quick inspection revealed that it could be repaired. Two porters were detailed to carry the boat down to the camp site and Rob, shivering and cold, adjourned to his tent to thaw out in his sleeping bag.

We had an early dinner that night. Tired and hungry, we ate ravenously, devouring great plates of rice and *dahl*. Afterwards we heard Mick's version of the accident:

It was the end of a long day and it was a classic example of tiredness and complacency. I was following Rob down a medium-sized rapid when I made the basic

118

mistake of reacting too slowly. Rob hit a stopper, capsized and instead of edging away from the stopper, I hit it head on and went over. I rolled late and drifted broadside on to a rock and capsized again leaning upstream. The pressure of the water forced me on to the back deck of the canoe and I was stuck there, unable to loose the spraysheet or get out of the canoe.

I tried for what seemed ages and eventually gave up in every sense of the word; at which point the boat for some reason or another came off and I managed to fight my way out in what I can only describe as panic. The boat appeared in front of me and I grabbed it but only for a short period of time, as I was swept downriver. I think swimming is a rather generous description – floating is a better expression – as I had been underneath for so long that I was totally unable to swim. I drifted past everyone on the bank and Mike (J) came racing across. I grabbed his boat and got a couple of breaths, but within a few seconds was swept away from the canoe.

I went round the corner and into the canyon, at which point I disappeared as the water built up against the bank and I was submerged for what seemed like an eternity. I fought for the surface and reappeared and fortunately Mike reappeared as well. He was still shouting at me to swim which I was completely incapable of doing. I was just getting battered along the bottom. Eventually he towed me into the right-hand bank and I grabbed hold of a rock, and just hung on, but if he hadn't got out of his boat quickly and given me his hand I would have just drifted off down the river again. I think that's the nearest I've ever been to drowning.

To bed at nine pm and, with Cat Stevens on the cassette, drifted off into a deep sleep.

9

Down the Rapids

THE NEXT MORNING DAWNED bright and clear. For once there had been no overnight rain and the sky was a perfect azure blue. I felt exhausted from the previous day's canoeing – walking is no exercise for the arm muscles. Mick appeared looking drawn and dishevelled. On his swim down the river he had been swept over and against innumerable submerged boulders and was stiff and aching. He was determined to go on the water and whilst breakfast was made ready, began fitting out one of the spare canoes. We were running low on serviceable boats. Mick used carpet tape to seal up several small cracks in the hull and deck.

On big water it is essential to secure a tight fit and wedge yourself snugly into the canoe by having the footrest against which you brace your feet at the right distance. He messed around for some minutes until he was finally satisfied that he had got the right position and then put the finishing touches to the canoe by writing 'Mick Hopkinson Mk II' with felt-tipped pen on the stern deck.

Annoyed at having lost his Prijon paddles, he checked the replacement pair. It is vitally important to have a reliable paddle and should it break on a rapid, the canoeist is left at the mercy of the river.

Breakfast was a leisurely affair as we planned the day's canoeing. Leo was determined to get on film the whole team shooting the rapid Mick had swum down and after some discussion we decided to portage back up to the rapid, shoot it and then drop back down again to the previous day's finishing point.

I volunteered to take the underwater camera on the canoe and began bolting it on to the front mounting. Leo loaded it and whilst he checked the alignment I experimented with the triggering device, which consisted of a small, match-box-sized control box. Its location was important since the cassette camera had little more than one minute's filming time and to ensure we got the maximum film, it had to be switched on as we were under way – quite a hair-raising experience. I was keen to put it in a position where I could hit it quickly, whilst leaving go of my paddles for the mini-mum length of time.

We were at the rapid by eight thirty am. The sun was climbing into the valley and everything glistened and sparkled as it hit the frothing river. More delays as Leo set his camera up and then we were ready for the off. It was the first time I had paddled with the underwater housing on and at once realised how unmanageable it made things. We edged into an eddy and sat bobbing up and down waiting to start. At last Leo dropped his hand, the signal for the off, and we edged into the current.

I dropped my paddle, fumbled for the switch and then paddled hard. I led, trying to take a left-hand route and avoid the worst of the stoppers we had gone through the previous day.

It was so different from yesterday. All I had to do then was concentrate on my own canoeing. Now the front end dug in badly and I half wondered if the camera would be capable of producing any worthwhile film for all this effort. We had been in such a rush leaving England that we had been unable to test it out beforehand.

I edged to the left to miss a rock and dropped into a huge stopper. Putting all my weight behind the right-hand blade of the paddle, I pulled hard on the wall of the stopper to break through. The front end reared madly in the air in a crazy loop. I swore loudly as it hung poised in a vertical position for a fraction of a second before crashing down-wards, fortunately clear of the stopper.

I pulled hard to the right following the route down which Mick had swum. I was determined to avoid any more stoppers whilst I had the camera on the canoe and took a line through a series of creamy-topped breaking waves. After 200 yards the rapid was slackening in pace. I pulled the canoe into the same break-out from which Mick had been rescued the previous day. Mick, looking relieved at having come down upright and in one piece, pulled in beside me, closely followed by Dave. Roger Huyton capsized ten yards upstream and was swept past as he missed his first roll and came up on his second attempt, to make a break-out a boat-length downstream of our position. John Liddell and Rob Hastings hit the eddy at the same time and their canoes crashed together as they manoeuvred into the slack water.

'How's the camera doing?' Roger called out.

'It's a good thing it's not a sound camera,' I replied, 'otherwise the way I was swearing up there would probably have me struck off the Medical Register. It really does make the canoe bloody unmanageable.'

Hoisting the canoes up, as we had little intention of shooting the section Rob and I had canoed the previous day, we left them for the porters to carry and headed back down to the point by the camp site where we had pulled out the previous afternoon.

Warming up with steaming hot brown mugs of tea, we watched Roger and Rob repairing the damaged canoes. Roger's seam, the point where the deck and hull are joined, had split wide open for over four feet behind the cockpit. He patiently wedged the two halves apart to dry, before sticking them together with long strips of plastic self-adhesive tape.

Leo was flitting around recovering film from the underwater camera and checking the mountings on the canoe. At last all was ready.

A large crowd had gathered on the bridge and the sun was beating down through a cloudless sky.

Sliding the canoes into the river, we strapped in and waited for the signal from Mick Reynolds. One of the cameras was not working well and there was some delay as one of the porters was sent racing back to the cook tent to collect a vital missing part.

A red handkerchief at last fluttered in the breeze and I broke out into the current. The camera was still bolted on to my canoe and the chatter from the motor was drowned as I hit the main stream. A piece of tape added as an afterthought by Leo to steady the camera, came loose and flapped in front of the lens. The canoe bucketed madly down a series of waves, crawling to the top and then accelerating as it went down the other side.

On my right a giant curling wave came screaming in and I braced madly as it crashed down on top of me. I felt the boat submerging and grabbed a lungful of air before going over in the ice cold water. It is a strange frightening world being swept along out of control at over thirty miles per hour. There is no more thundering noise, just murky, swirling water in this crazy, topsy-turvy world of the capsized canoeist. Mechanically the paddles go into place, sweep around and I lever the canoe upright, rapidly clear my eyes and decide on a line down the next section of river.

We made slow progress through the morning. Each rapid was carefully inspected and surveyed; we were reluctant to take any big risks. After Mick's experience the previous day we all realised how desperate a swim could be.

Despite his accident Mick rapidly recovered his confidence and in his 'Mick Hopkinson Mk II' was in fine form, shooting and leading down some formidable rapids.

By one pm we reached an interesting section where a forty-foot log was jammed across the river. Dave Manby, Roger Huyton and I were on the left-hand bank, Rob Hastings and Mick Hopkinson were on the right.

The entire flow was directed against the tree trunk with only a small, three-foot gap for the canoe to squeeze through. To be trapped against the tree and caught in its branches would be fatal.

Leo, high up on a bluff overlooking the rapid, had already positioned his cameras waiting for the excitement. To hit the gap would require a tremendous amount of skill and strength to break through the stoppers above it, and a considerable amount of luck.

I rapidly made up my mind and floated my canoe down the small eddies on the left-hand bank, bypassing the obstacle and re-launching below it. Dave and Roger followed suit. On the far bank Rob and Mick seemed undecided but eventually they, too, made up their minds to portage, much to Leo's annoyance since he had been waiting for over two hours for the action shots.

We continued down, crossing from one side of the river to the other as we picked our way down the rapids.

It was hard, sustained canoeing, exciting and exhilarating. We were all paddling well and glided effortlessly down rapid after rapid, becoming accustomed to the speed of the water.

Whilst we paddled John Gosling was busy stripping and dismantling our camp site at Phakding and moving it eight miles downstream to Ghat, where we intended camping that evening. From Ghat he wanted to go to Luglha to check the airfield down to Kharikhola and to fetch up essential foodstuffs which we had stored there.

We were still two miles above Ghat and by three pm, cold and exhausted by eight hours' canoeing, we arrived at the last rapid we would shoot before leaving the canoes on the bank and dropping down to the camp site. It consisted of two large, ten-foot-high waterfalls, separated by a section of thirty feet or so of broken water.

Mick shot it on the left, I bumbled through on the right and Rob set off to go down the centre. We watched horrified as he was caught in a stopper above the first fall and capsized. There was no time to roll and his canoe was swept upside down over the first ten-foot drop, and within a few seconds over the second. We felt helpless as the canoe cleared the stopper at the bottom of the fall and crunched into a rock. Panic gripped me momentarily as I imagined that Rob had been swept out of the boat and was swimming, and then to my relief a paddle appeared and Rob rolled the canoe upright, with no more than a series of deep scratches on his crash helmet where he had been crashed against submerged rocks.

It had been a lucky escape, as Rob told us afterwards. He realised when he went over at the top of the first fall that he did not have time to roll up before the second one so he just wedged himself into the canoe as tightly as possible and held his breath as he went over both. It had required a cool head and nerves of steel and strengthened my admiration for Rob, who was doing a tremendous amount of the canoe leading.

The tents were pitched at Ghat in a small, grassy field by the side of a teahouse and we sat and talked absorbing the last few rays of a gleaming coppery sun as it sank over the distant mountains.

Leo was entertaining himself tackling a small boulder problem, an almost smooth slab no more than fifteen feet high, which he was delicately balancing up. We burst out laughing as he fell off time and time again. Was this really Leo Dickinson, the great mountaineer and climber who had climbed the Eiger and Matterhorn? The more we laughed, the more annoyed Leo became until eventually, hot and bothered, he resigned himself to sitting on a stone at the foot of the climb and staring up at the smooth expanse of rock.

Jimmy, our fifteen-year-old cook, decided to have a go and in full view of an amazed crowd, balanced his way up to the top of the rock. It was just too much for Leo who later that night was seen attacking the rock with ice-hammer and pitons to prove that he, too, could scale it.

That night I sat alone in my tent and pored over figures, calculations and dates that I had in my diary. We were running out of boats, and those boats that were left had taken a severe battering and required considerable fibreglass repair work to make them usable.

We were running out of time. It was now September 23rd, and we had planned to be back in England by October 1st. There were commitments back home. Work, jobs, university and college courses. It already seemed even to the most optimistic team members that we would be over a month late.

In addition we were running out of fit people to paddle the canoes and over half the team was out of action with one thing or another.

But the most important and worrying aspect of the expedition was the financial one. We had gone considerably over our budget and now were more than £3,000 in the red and we were still only halfway through the trip.

I sat and pondered, juggling the possibilities and alternatives in my mind.

My biggest headache was deciding how the canoeists would be supported from the bank on the stretch from

Jubing down to the confluence, if the trail along the gorge was, as the porters said, virtually impossible to walk, since it had been swept away by many landslips that winter and not repaired. If that was the case, we would have to finish at Jubing and walk out from there, as we did not have the resources to carry on down to the Sun Kosi without bank support.

I decided late that night to set out at first light the following day and walk to Kharikhola, compressing two days' walk into one, and the following day survey the track and river below Jubing. Meanwhile the rest of the team would continue canoeing with a major portage around a particularly severe gorge above Jubing, where I would meet them in three days.

Over breakfast the following day I told the team of my decision and watched them start canoeing before leaving for Kharikhola. I walked hard and fast and arrived at the village by four that afternoon. John Gosling was there, having walked from Luglha where he had been the day before to check the arrival of any planes. I told him of my plans and he agreed to continue down with me.

There were three young Swedish trekkers and we ate and drank with our new-found friends until eventually we curled up in the smoke-filled atmosphere of the teahouse and fell into an exhausted sleep.

John woke me at five am and in the pale, half-light of dawn we left Kharikhola and slipped down to Jubing. The river level was falling rapidly and had dropped over eight feet since we had crossed the bridge on the way in. Numerous razor-sharp rocks were now visible in the water.

We climbed up the valley side and spent a fruitless two hours searching for the trail that would take us towards the Sun Kosi. It was stifling hot as we waded through paddy fields, stopping every few minutes to pick the eternal blood-sucking leeches from arms and legs.

At last – exhausted, dishevelled and tired – we stumbled on to the trail. It was a far cry from the well-trodden track we had come to know and at times disappeared completely as we picked our way across landslides and through dense undergrowth.

It was hard going. At one place a landslip had taken over fifty yards of the path away and we balanced ourselves across an eighty degree scree slope with precious little between us and the river over 1,000 feet below.

Even from that height, it looked ferocious and by midday we had decided the porters would never agree to the dangerous carry along the trail.

My mind was made up and we sat in the shade of a cliff blissfully dangling our tired and aching feet in a sparkling mountain stream, which fell rapidly to the river below. I spoke my thoughts out aloud.

'It's obvious we can't have bank support from Jubing down and I think we might as well call it a day at the bridge and get back to Kathmandu. We've done our best.'

We pushed hard back to Jubing and arrived a few minutes ahead of the main party. I told them what we had found and the decision to go back to Kathmandu. We had, after all, descended forty miles of the toughest gradient in the world.

Their reaction was as I expected. Partly disappointment at not being able to complete the forty miles of the rest of the river, tinged with a sense of relief at not having to live on nerves as we tackled more rapids.

Working late into the night we reorganised the loads for the two parties. At last everything was ready. Leo wanted some film of us canoeing under the bridge at Jubing and the next morning we intended shooting the final rapid before heading back to Kathmandu.

10

A Change of Plan

It was Saturday, September 25th and today was our last on the river. The kettle was simmering on a crackling wood fire as I lazed on a rock, absorbing the warmth from the early morning sun as it crept into the Dudh Kosi valley. I pondered about the day ahead.

We were fast running out of money as we were spending over forty pounds a day on porters. Most of the canoes were now broken or in poor shape, covered in patches. We looked a sorry lot with our swollen, peeling, sun-scorched faces; many of us had raw suppurating sores and cracked blistered lips. We were badly in need of a rest and more nutritious food. So I felt that I had taken the correct decision when I had made up my mind to return to Kathmandu without canoeing down the last part of the river to its confluence with the Sun Kosi. The previous night I had also decided to speed up our departure by splitting the team into two parties for the walk out: a fast-moving group to get things organised in Kathmandu and a slower party made up of those not in a hurry.

Mick Hopkinson would come in the first group with me, Rob Hastings, John Gosling and Pancho, our second sirdar. We planned to reach Kathmandu in four days, less than half the time it had taken us to walk the ninety miles on the way in. The remainder of the team, together with the porters, would be walking out at the normal, leisurely pace, giving me an extra few days before they arrived to cable for more finance, file press reports, organise airflights for Rob Hastings who was already overdue for a teacher training course in England, and one for John Liddell who was desperately in need of a rest and in no fit state to embark upon the marathon drive home, as well as clearing up the

128

thousand and one bits and pieces which needed to be done before we left Kathmandu.

Mick Hopkinson, ever industrious, was repairing his canoe and I wandered across and pulled my boat into the sun and inspected its hull. It was rapidly being broken up by the enormous pressure waves generated on the rapids and I wedged open two large cracks in the hull with small sticks, since we had found that to get the repair tape to take and make a waterproof mend, it was vitally important to have the fibre-glass bone dry.

I collected my camera from the tent whilst the boat heated up in the bright sunlight and returned to my rocky perch. Never very mechanically-minded, I spent ten minutes re-loading the camera, patiently slotting a film into the gate before it finally caught and tensioned on the wind-on spool.

John Liddell had appeared next to me and delivered a bundle of letters for me to post in Kathmandu. He sat down and, wearing a worried frown on his face, sifted through several sheets of closely-packed figures and calculations. Finally with a flourish of his pen he completed his computations and spoke.

'You'll never believe this,' he said, 'but we have spent over £2,500 on porters and we only budgeted for £800.'

To John's amazement I was delighted and said so. 'That's great news. I worked out last night it was £3,000!'

In fact by the time we had paid porter perks and backsheesh, my figure was to be nearer the final portering bill and once again I had learnt the hard way that expedition budgets require much foresight, generous allowances and estimates for the imponderables and improbables, and a cool head and understanding bank manager when things go wrong.

A group of porters and locals were gathered round the teahouse, waiting patiently for me to run a morning clinic. Rescuing my medical bag out of one of the tall, wicker carrying baskets, I set up a rough and ready surgery on the rocks and treated a never-ending stream of cuts, bruises, skin ulcers and minor trivia, dishing out pills, plasters and words of advice. I strongly disapproved of dishing out pills at random to any Sherpa who chanced to come by, for I felt that sporadic medical attention by passing doctors such as myself was worse than no medical treatment at all. But I was willing to help those locals who were part of our own expedition, and to treat those who had been injured whilst portering for us.

The shout went up for breakfast and we ambled across to the cook tent. Everyone was keyed up and excited at the prospect of finishing the river and we ate a hurried meal. By eight thirty am everything was ready and the patched-up canoes were despatched to the rapids. The whole team was going on the water and we walked down the trail discussing what we would do once we got back to civilisation. Food seemed to be the main topic and steak and chips the number one choice for a first meal once we got back to Kathmandu.

But there was still canoeing to be done and we clambered through brambles and thigh-clinging undergrowth to in- spect the fall. The nervous tension was running high, as we viewed the rapid in excited anticipation. Both Leo and Mick Reynolds were dashing to and fro, positioning tripods and cameras for the finishing shot. Viewed from below, the fall looked enormous and there appeared to be only one line down on the right-hand bank, where a water shoot dropped ten feet or so into an enormous churning stopper and then turned through ninety degrees to drop down a smaller shoot into a second stopper. It looked grade-six canoeing and I was anxious to avoid any accidents in the final stages of the expedition. I spoke to Mick and we con- sidered launching below the fall but, after looking at the chute from above, rejected the idea and I hauled my canoe to the water's edge, lowered it into the water and eased myself into the cockpit.

It was perilous stuff; the canoe crashed and jarred against the partly submerged rocks as the river rose and fell. At last I managed to clip the spraysheet on and pushing off from the side spun the canoe around to face upstream and, paddling hard, angled across to the opposite bank. Even after two weeks on the river the speed of the water caught me by surprise and I found myself making little headway and rapidly being swept towards the impossible section of the fall, where the river dropped fifteen feet on to the rocks below. I stroked frantically and powered the canoe across and with a foot to spare made the chute. Fighting to regain control, I straightened up as the canoe gathered momentum in the chute before hitting the stopper and jarring to a halt, as it collided head on with a rock hidden in the wall of white water. My feet slammed into the footrest and the whole canoe shuddered as the water submerged the stern deck and for one minute I thought I was going to loop as the bow started rising in the air. I dug my paddle into the wave face and pulled hard and the canoe slowly rode up over the wave and out of danger.

There was little time to recover, as the canoe headed towards the thirty-foot-long rock face against which the whole strength of the river seemed to be directed. Reversing madly I backed away, clipped the very end of the face and, spotting a small shoot running through the second stopper, powered through it. I broke out beneath the fall and watched the rest of the team come through. It was a difficult fall. Dave Manby capsized but made an excellent recovery. John, Rob and Mick sailed down in fine style; Roger just bumbled through. Leo came racing down the bank, movie camera strapped to his shoulder and film chattering through the gate, making us all feel like Hollywood movie stars as he shot close-ups of our elated faces. Canoes were hauled to the path, wet and soggy gear hung out to dry before packing it into canoes for the carry back to Kathmandu.

Secretly, I was terribly disappointed at not having succeeded in shooting the whole river. Leo was alone on the bridge, dismantling his camera gear and I strolled across to him. We talked the matter over. He too was disappointed that we had not completed the river and, more important, was concerned with the weak ending to the film, which might upset our sponsors who had spent so many thousands of pounds on the project.

We changed into dry shorts and T-shirts and stood around warming up, sipping steaming mugs of tea and eating Ryvitas and marmalade until we bid our farewells and started the tortuous ascent out of the Dudh Kosi gorge.

Mick Hopkinson voiced my thoughts as we climbed up in the oppressive oven-like heat, 'You know,' he said, 'that's the second time we've left a river half done.'

He was referring to our Blue Nile expedition when we had abandoned the expedition after two hundred and twenty miles, and only completed half of the distance we had intended doing.

I hate failure and that remark triggered my intention to look at ways of finishing the lower section of the river as soon as we got back to Kathmandu.

Setting a cracking pace, carrying no food or camping gear and with nothing more than the clothes we stood up in and a sleeping bag, we covered two stages to reach Junbesi by nightfall.

There was a distinct competitive element as we took it in turns to lead and force the pace, sweating up hills and racing down the other side.

We had not eaten all day and sat down to demolish enormous plates piled high with potatoes and, of all things, spinach. It was delicious and, with our sleeping bags laid out on the airy verandah, well satisfied we collapsed into a deep sleep.

Before sun-up and in the half-light of dawn we picked our way through the village, past sleeping dogs and on to the trail. By seven thirty am, we were climbing up an 11,000-foot pass and we pushed on, remembering the small building just past the summit where we had eaten freshly-made goat cheese and drunk delicious, creamy tea. Alas, we arrived to find the building abandoned and the goat herd gone to lower pastures, so we went on until we came to a small village where we rested in a fly-ridden tea house and ordered breakfast.

It was remarkable how the rivers had dropped with the end of the monsoon. No longer were they the churning, thundering torrents I remembered on the way in, but slow, meandering waterways with pools and shallows. The whole countryside was coming alive: men were at work in the fields and women sat by their open doors pounding the millet to make *tsampa*. Even the children worked, carrying colossal loads in from the fields and tending the animals.

By two pm it was blistering hot and we stopped by the side of a mountain stream. Rob stripped off and dived into the ice cold water to wash off the grime and filth accumulated over the last two days.

A spindly-legged youth of sixteen or so came racing down the hill and we watched as he leapt expertly from rock to rock. It was the mail runner who had been sent back to Kathmandu and we called out to him. He came over with beads of perspiration on his forehead, sat down and emptied his mail bag on to a small rock. There was the money for John Liddell to pay the porters and bundles of letters from friends and relatives back in England. After being absorbed in the news from home, at last we stirred and waved the runner on his way, before beginning the long haul up the next peak.

Three stages is no mean feat but we covered them by sunset and, almost too exhausted to eat, collapsed in an airy teahouse and fell into an untroubled sleep.

This was the halfway point on our walk out and the next day, following the same routine of leaving before sunrise and walking constantly through the heat of the day, we made good time. At five thirty pm we found ourselves benighted in a deep river valley with no signs of habitation. With a solitary pen-torch shared between five people, we picked our way through the inky blackness to a small collection of houses, where we bartered for eggs and potatoes. Pancho cooked these on an iron grill set over the hearth.

Aching with exhaustion we talked excitedly of Kathmandu, steak and chips, clean white sheets and a comfortable bed which would be ours once we reached civilisation.

By five am we were away, making fast time so that by midday we were within eight miles of Lamosangu, the point at which we had started the walk in to Base Camp Everest. The daily bus from Lamosangu to Kathmandu leaves at four pm and we were determined to catch it and enjoy the luxuries of a slap-up meal and bed that night.

Everything was going well when three miles from Lamosangu John Gosling tripped and fell, badly spraining his right ankle. There was nothing to be done except offer

133

sympathy and commiserate with him, and solely intent on catching the bus, we abandoned him to the care of Pancho. Racing on, we shouted back to John that we would eat his steak and chips for him if he missed the four pm deadline. Wryly he joined in our amusement.

As we neared the town we came across increasing numbers of townsfolk wearing bright, flowery summer dresses and smart, lightweight suits, on their way to the mountains to visit families and relatives for the Buddhist New Year festivities, which take place in late September.

We arrived at Lamosangu with twenty minutes to spare, crowded on to a bench outside a teashop and emptied bottle after bottle of Coke and lemonade. At last the bus driver clambered aboard and we piled in after him, stacking our rucksacks on the back seat.

It was an old, rattling bus and apart from our group of three, there were a dozen other passengers, in addition to a goat which was tethered in the centre aisle and twenty or so clucking and squawking hens in rough, mesh wire cases stacked on the seats.

The engine roared, throwing out great clouds of black smoke through the tail pipe, and there was a crash as the driver engaged first gear and we rumbled forward. Up the hill above the town the two bright red rucksacks of Gosling and Pancho were just visible and we chuckled at the thought of them spending another night eating rice and *dahl* and sleeping in fly-ridden houses, and missing out on our feast in Kathmandu.

Rattling and lurching alarmingly, we raced along beside the Sun Kosi, the driver spinning the massive steering wheel between his hands and gunning the engine as he changed from one gear to the next.

After an hour on the road there was a sudden pop and a hiss, and a cloud of dense blue-black smoke came billowing from the direction of the engine as we groaned to a halt.

The driver leapt out of his cab, threw open the bonnet and with a fistful of spanners disappeared into the engine. Intrigued and morose, we watched as first one bit of the motor was removed and then another. Eventually the driver looked resigned, threw his arms in the air, closed the engine compartment and set off up the road. One of the bus occupants made out in sign language that we should sleep by the side of the road and the bus would be repaired the following day.

How the tables had turned! Now John Gosling was the envy of everyone as he sat in a *chi* house* in Lamosangu, eating rice and *dahl* and drinking Coke. We had nothing to eat or drink and nowhere to stay.

Suddenly there was a commotion as with a hoot, a workmen's bus came careering and skidding around the corner and there, sitting in the front seat like a lord, was Gosling, eating his way through a bunch of fifty or so bananas.

Smirking all over his face, he invited us aboard his relief bus whilst both drivers checked out our broken engine.

'So you thought you'd left me behind,' he joked. 'You know, you went off in such a bloody rush you didn't leave me with any money and I've had to borrow the bus fare off one of our porters I bumped into in the village.'

Apparently he had missed our bus by ten minutes and had resigned himself to another miserable night in Lamosangu, when a bus fetching workmen from repairing the road above the town had suddenly appeared and he had hitched a ride with little trouble. Apparently our engine was irreparably damaged and, leaving our bus, we all clambered aboard the replacement, arriving in Kathmandu by ten pm. We immediately hailed two taxis and headed for the Hotel Asia, where we gorged ourselves and talked late into the night.

I was awake by seven am and lay in bed savouring the delights of clean sheets and a soft mattress. I felt uneasy. Had we done the right thing walking out, would the expedition be seen as a failure once we got back to England? A cool breeze blew through the open windows and the sun slanted down between the slats of the shutters which swung gently on their mountings.

My mind was fresh, uncluttered with the day-to-day problems which had occupied me for the last month and I threw ideas around until eventually I reached a solution.

It was important from the story and film point of view to

finish the river. It was obviously impossible to go back in as a heavyweight expedition with porters and bank support as we had done on the top section. The alternative was to go in as a lightweight, self-contained group, carrying food and sleeping bags in the canoes and descend the river sleeping in the open on the bank. The idea appealed to me, as Mick Hopkinson and I had shot the Blue Nile in this way, and there was no reason why it would not work on the Dudh Kosi. Since the monsoon had now finished and the water was dropping daily, I was confident that with the lower gradient on the bottom section we could descend the forty or so miles to the confluence in two to three days.

There still remained the problem of getting back onto the river. To repair canoes, rest up and get back into shape would take at least a week, a week to walk back in and a further two to canoe and come out; in total a month which was utterly impractical. I puzzled over my plan. The whole scheme fell down because of the time taken to get back into the river. And then I had it. Why not fly in? The monsoon was ending and the hundreds of small grass air-strips dotted all over Nepal would be opening up once their fields dried out. Better still, why not helicopter in carrying the canoes slung underneath? The whole scale of things was taking on the size of a major motion picture. Excited at the prospect of finishing the river off, I showered, dressed and breakfasted.

Our Transit van was still waiting to be repaired and whilst Rob and Mick set to work on it, I spent the morning trying to get hold of Mike Cheney. Eventually at one pm I located him and drove across to his house, where he listened intently as I recounted our adventures and followed up with my plans to go back in again. He seemed baffled at first as to why we should want to go back but agreed to help. A map of the lower Dudh Kosi was produced and we studied it closely.

We looked carefully at the lower section. One of the alternatives open to us was to walk in to the confluence of the Sun and Dudh Kosi and work our way upstream, surveying the river as we walked up it before canoeing down. There was a dirt track road approximately eighty miles south of the junction of the two rivers and providing we could drive along it we would have a three-day walk in.

My finger traced the tortuous course of the river and came to rest on a small air-strip at Lamindamba and I wondered whether we would be able to fly the boats in there.

I felt indecisive as I left Mike Cheney's, but late that night made the decision to go all out for a light aircraft to fly into Lamindamba.

The next four days went in a whirlwind of activity. On Thursday evening Mick and Rob drove up to Lamosangu to meet the main party when they arrived, which we speculated would probably be on the following day.

Meanwhile, I wheeled and dealed trying to organise a flight in. Aeroplanes in Nepal are few and far between and with the end of the wet season most were fully booked up, ferrying much-needed supplies to mountain villages. At last a ray of hope and I provisionally booked a flight for the Tuesday afternoon.

The airport had by now closed down for the New Year celebrations and, resolving to join in the festivities, I returned to the hotel to find that the main party had just arrived. They looked tired and haggard and, giving them a few minutes to recover, I took Leo aside and told him of my progress. He was pleasantly surprised since this would give him an ending to the film, but insisted we ought to have a team meeting and full discussion.

We met in my bedroom and in a tense atmosphere, I explained my plans to go back into the river. Even Mick Hopkinson, who should have understood my thinking more than anyone else, was surprised but my mind was made up and at the end of the meeting my decision had been endorsed. Since only two canoes could be carried in the plane, I asked Mick Hopkinson to accompany me.

The weekend passed in an alcoholic haze. Shops were closed, there was dancing in the streets and goats were ceremoniously sacrificed in the market place. Relishing our return to civilisation, we joined in with fervour and energy.

On Monday morning we drove out to the airport and, carrying two repaired canoes, made our way across to the perimeter of the air-strip where our Pilatus aircraft was parked.

It was a small six-seater and I was dubious about our canoes fitting in. A mechanic came across and slid the side door open for us. Looking inside, the cockpit was barely eight feet long with a hinged flap at the rear, which looked as though it would swing up and give us an extra few feet. The mechanic explained in broken English that once the seats were taken out the canoes could be eased in without any problems. I only wished I shared his confidence. There was no time to try a test run fitting the canoes into the plane, as it was being prepared for take off and the boats had already been loaded on to a baggage trolley and wheeled into a hangar.

As I returned to the hotel, I was thinking of the time in Cairo when the porters tried, the stewards tried, and eventually the helpful pilot and I tried to get my canoe into the hold of the fabulous Comet to go to Addis Ababa. It was just like one of those ridiculously frustrating children's puzzles, you felt that if you could only find the right position or the right angle, you would succeed. A marvellous aircraft, but after our vain efforts, it was obvious that the designer had never considered the problem of getting a sleek, fourteen-foot racing kayak into its hold. To think of it, perhaps aircraft designers don't like boats. Anyway, I now have an in-built suspicion of the carrying capacity of any aircraft.

Back to reality; it was a kind of limbo period, just waiting for the off with little incentive to read and pointless to write home with our news until we could say that we had finished the river.

Mick Hopkinson had organised the small quantity of food we were taking in a rucksack. There were half a dozen or so Mars Bars, a tinned Dundee cake, a packet of raisins and a few cans of sardines and kippers. We were desperately trying to keep the weight of gear in the canoes down but with the mass of camera equipment and film, in addition to sleeping bags and a few essential items of spare clothing, we already had over thirty pounds each.

Totally unprepared for carrying gear in the canoes, we

cannibalised the waterproof coverings from the remaining food boxes and used these to pack our luggage into.

Tuesday, October 4th.

I woke and opened the shutters to gaze out over the flat rooftops of Kathmandu. There was a low cloud ceiling and the weather was dull and oppressive. Yesterday most of the afternoon flights had been cancelled by torrential thunderstorms, which made landing on grass air-strips a risky business.

A few drops of rain pattered on the galvanised tin roof and splashed on the windowpane and I resigned myself to another day in the hotel.

Suddenly someone was shaking me violently by the shoulder. I had fallen asleep and now it was past ten am and the sun was beginning to break through the heavy monsoon clouds. I showered, dressed and raced downstairs to where a taxi was waiting to take us to the airport.

We were there by midday and sat in the airport lounge drinking expensive coffee and watching the flights come and go. At two pm, our departure time, the flight had not been called and by three pm there was still no announcement. I wandered across to the flight desk but despite my enquiries there was no news.

A middle-aged, heavily-built man with a bronzed, cheerful face came over and introduced himself as Emil Wick, our pilot. He apologised for the delay, speaking in a thick German accent.

'I'm sorry, boys, but the weather is breaking up and we'll have to postpone your flight. Come first thing in the morning and we'll try again.'

Bitterly disappointed, we drove back to the hotel. More delays, waiting around and more boredom.

The Kathmandu bazaar was open. There was a mass of things to choose from ranging from beautiful hand-woven tapestries, delicately-carved wooden ornaments, beaten copper trays and vases, and long, curved Ghurka knives. I spent the remainder of the day shopping for presents to take home to relatives and friends back in England. Eating in a local restaurant, we were surprised to find that all the prices had almost doubled. We queried the price-rise with the restaurant owner. 'You know,' he said, 'it's the start of another tourist season and we always double our prices and the Americans still think they're eating cheaply!'

We left early and were ready for bed by ten pm. Before turning in I looked out at the sky. It was streaked bright red and I hoped that this was a good sign for the following day's weather.

Mick Hopkinson woke me at six thirty am and by seven thirty we were on our way to the airport. It was warm and a few mackerel clouds scudding over the hills in the west boded well for the day ahead.

In the airport lounge we ordered an English breakfast and tucked into eggs and bacon, hot buttered toast and steaming black coffee. Emil Wick was sitting with a group of pilots and I crossed over to him.

'Do you think we will get off today?' I enquired.

He nodded. 'I hope so. Listen to the loudspeaker as one of my flights has been cancelled this morning and you might get that slot.'

We sat drinking coffee and reading the newspapers. There was nothing particularly interesting, mostly government news, although there was a brief report from the American Everest expedition saying that they were now well established on the face and would be making a summit bid in the next few days.

At ten thirty am Emil Wick stuck his head around the door.

'Come on, you're off,' he called out.

We scrambled, checked out through security and walked across the tarmac to where the Pilatus was parked. The canoes were waiting to be slotted in and the mechanic was already busily unbolting seats from their runners and sliding them out.

Not over optimistic, I had brought a hacksaw and two rolls of tape. If they failed to fit in I was simply going to saw the excess off and stick it back on with tape when we got to Lamindamba.

The pilot and mechanic disappeared to the hangar whilst Mick and I continued loading the canoes into the plane. Forgetting that we were dealing with over a quarter of a million pounds' worth of aeroplane, we pushed and tugged as we tried to ease the first canoe into the aircraft. At last it slotted into place.

The second was no easier and, sweating and straining, we tried to coax it into the confined fuselage. There was no way we could make it fit until Mick Hopkinson, deciding brute strength was the only possible course of action, grabbed hold of the joy stick, put his size eleven boot against it and ignoring the intricate mechanism it controlled, levered it over a fraction of an inch, enabling us to nudge the second canoe into position.

We now had to slot the three seats into place since Leo was coming along to do some aerial photography and we managed to slot the first, then the second and finally the last into position.

'OK,' called the pilot, 'let's go.'

The passenger door slammed, seat belts were locked and tightened, and the engine started. Taxiing to the edge of the air-field we waited for clearance to take off. There was a mass of cotton wool clouds moving in rapidly from the west.

'Looks like you've just made it in time,' observed the pilot.

The engine roared and the whole plane vibrated, and with the wing tips slicing through the air, we accelerated down the runway. We were off.

11

The Two-man Push

THE SUN GLINTED ON the plane's windscreen as it climbed into the sky. An ever widening vista of hills, mountains and open country spread out in front of us. The aircraft banked and held 9,000 feet as it raced over the tin-roofed houses of Kathmandu and towards the low-lying hills in the north.

Climbing again and noses flattened against the Perspex windows, squinting downwards as we crossed green, terraced paddy fields, over a man and oxen laboriously ploughing a small plot of land and a group of workers thatching a cottage. Hitting an air pocket the aircraft lurched and suddenly dropped; momentarily my pulse quickened as the canoes slid forward and jammed against the rudder bar. I held on and slid them back tightening the tapes holding them in position as we regained height.

Our pilot, Emil Wick, pulled a packet of Gauloises from his shirt breast pocket, slid one of the cigarettes out and lit up as he scanned the horizon for landmarks. He had been in Nepal for over fourteen years and in that time had built up a considerable reputation as a skilful and dedicated pilot. On the 1960 Swiss expedition to Dhaulagiri, which in climbing difficulties ranks only just behind Everest, he had safely landed his plane on skis at 19,200 feet forty-two times to take in supplies and equipment. He had been unlucky on the forty-third landing, one of the skis snagging in a crevasse, resulting in the plane crashing and Wick, none the worse for wear, having to spend the better part of a week walking back to Kathmandu.

I already knew something about his reputation before we met at the airport. Just before we took off, one of the airport employees wandered up to me, no doubt imagining I was very nervous at the prospect of flying in such a small plane, and whispered in my ear, 'Don't worry. You're flying with a very lucky pilot; he's crashed three times but survived every time!' It did little to bolster my sagging confidence particularly as we climbed into the plane and I noticed that he was the only one wearing a parachute!

Swiftly he turned the plane to port, skirted a low bank of cloud and in the distance we saw the glistening waters of the Sun Kôsi. It snaked its way along the bottom of a wild, isolated valley. We flew along its course, using it as a landmark and navigation aid. Leo, sitting up front, was in his element triggering off short bursts of movie film at the landscape below.

The scenery was impressive: vast sweeping ridges, rounded bluffs and terraces carved into the hillside. For several miles the river gently meandered its way along the valley floor until constrictions in the rock bed compressed the water into huge standing waves and stoppers. Even from 3,000 feet above Mick Hopkinson claimed he could see enormous stoppers and falls and that was without his glasses! Tracing the course of the river, we strained to catch further glimpses of it through isolated windows in the layers of clouds which were forming below us.

I recalled that Liz Hawley from Reuters had told me that Ed Hillary, the Everest climber, was hoping to come upstream from the Ganges and into the Dudh Kosi in jet boats. I imagined that it would be an incredible ride up the rapids and provide fine action for the film and book he was going to produce, appropriately named *From the Ocean to the Sky*.

I ran out several frames of film and decided one day to organise my own expedition down the river.

Occasionally we saw enormous shingle banks, a sure sign that the river was going down, although the monsoon rains had only ended the week before.

Glancing at my watch, I saw that we had been airborne for over an hour and wondered how much further before we saw the confluence of the Sun and Dudh Kosi. As if he had sensed my impatience, the pilot tapped on the window and pointed downwards to where two river valleys merged.

'Is that it?' I shouted above the roar of the engines. He nodded and swooped low, circling the swirling, milky waters of the Dudh Kosi as they emptied into the grey of the Sun.

The Dudh Kosi valley stretched away in front of us. It was a rugged, steeply-cut valley with precipitous cliff faces running down to the water's edge. Several isolated houses were built high up on the valleysides.

We flew upstream, anxiously scanning the river. To fall out of one's canoe in the ice-cold water would not only involve a difficult and dangerous swim to the bank, but skilful rock climbing to get out of the water. In places there would be no hope of getting the canoe out, since the cliff ran straight into the river which raced past at a frightening speed. Later we were to find that in many places the cliffs were undercut by the current, which had scalloped out and worn away underground cave systems from which there was no hope of a swimmer escaping. In Kathmandu we had heard of crocodiles in the Sun Kosi, but hoped that the cold water of the Dudh Kosi would deter them from exploring its lower reaches. The crocodile is the most unsociable and dangerous animal to meet on the river, as I knew from the Blue Nile. A crocodile swiftly on the attack is capable of provoking thrilling and amazing performances out of the most tired and jaded of canoeists. It was an experience we were very willing to forgo.

It was an enormous relief to find that the rapids above the confluence were not as sustained as on the top section, with long stretches of flat, fast-moving water following each series of falls and rapids. This was as we expected, since the gradient in the lower section was very much less than in the upper part.

We rounded a bluff in the river and throttled back. Two miles ahead was a dark brown landing-strip carved into the hillside and angled at forty-five degrees uphill. It was less than 200 yards long by forty yards wide and a premature touchdown or overshoot would have been disastrous. The 'control tower' appeared to be a man dressed in blue overalls frantically waving two bright red batons.

'Jesus, we're not landing there, are we?' I called out to the

Tengpoche monastery.

A chance to assess the rapids of the Dudh Kosi at close quarters.

Eskimo rolling on a major Himalayan rapid. It's hard enough to get sufficient air into the lungs right side up at this altitude. If you lose contact with the canoe you're as good as dead.

pilot who was deftly throwing switches and adjusting levers. Obviously in his element, he grinned and called back, ' 'Fraid so, just hang on!'

I grabbed my seat belt and pulled it in three notches until it felt as though it was going to cut me in half and wedged the boats in tightly with my right leg.

The wind whistled through the ailerons as we glided in to land. Suddenly there was a surge of power as the propeller speed increased, the pilot pulled back on the joystick and we skimmed over the airfield and back into the sky.

My pulse was racing and I felt cold and clammy.

'Just a practice run to make sure there are no cows on the landing strip.' Emil banked around and came in again, gliding in to make a perfect text-book landing. I held on to my seat as we bucketed and bumped our way along the earth and rubble runway and, with the propeller spinning idly, taxied to a small hut on the edge of the airfield. The door slid open and, thankful to have survived, Mick Hopkinson and I climbed out.

An enormous crowd of locals gathered and chattered excitedly as the canoes were eased out and stacked beside the aircraft.

'Do you want some porters?' the pilot shouted above the noise of the crowd. I asked for four and they were singled out from the throng. Shouldering the canoes, with one at either end, they carried them out of the path of the aircraft.

Leo was keen to get some close-up shots of the river and we watched as the side door was fastened open and he positioned himself in a seat so that he could hang out into space through the open fuselage. The starter whirred and the engine coughed, spluttered and burst into a healthy roar. The plane taxied to the top of the runway and we watched expectantly as the engine reached a crescendo, and with the propeller grabbing the air, accelerated down the runway.

As it left the ground, Emil Wick, always one to play to the crowds, banked through ninety degrees so that the wing tip almost scraped the ground and, with a pale faced Leo desperately clinging to the fuselage, disappeared at an alarming angle towards the river.

The locals just loved it and burst out cheering. Mad dogs and Englishmen!

Our porters were ready to be off and, stacking equipment and food into the canoes, started down a hard-packed gravel track into the gorge.

After two hours' walking we stopped by a shady brook and, taking boots and socks off, dangled tired and aching feet in the crystal clear water. Pushing on we reached the river by two pm and relaxed inside a teahouse, away from the glare of the sun. We looked out over the Dudh Kosi which at this point was over fifty yards wide. Fast flowing, but with none of the major water or rock hazards we remembered so vividly from the top section.

Propping the canoes against a tree to dry out in the sun, we checked our equipment: a sleeping bag with large plastic orange bivouac sheet, a few Mars Bars and four assorted cans of sardines and kippers, and a mass of cameras and photographic gear.

'Where's the Dundee cake?' asked Mick.

'I haven't got it, you have,' I replied.

We both searched our boats but as we looked I remembered where it was – the lovely Dundee cake was underneath the pilot's seat on its way back to Kathmandu!

Everything was packed into large, heavy-duty fertiliser sacks which were sealed with tape and wedged back into the canoes.

At last all was ready, and with many helping hands the canoes were lowered into the rushing water. I set up a film sequence as Mick climbed aboard, fastened his spraysheet, checked his crash helmet and slipped downstream. The cassette ran out, so I changed it for a fresh one before easing myself into the cockpit, locking the camera between my thighs and following him downstream.

The sun blazed down through a cloudless sky and we drifted lazily with the current. Refreshed and rested after our week's stay in Kathmandu, it felt good to be back on the river again. Only forty miles to go. Embarking upon the ultimate in canoe adventure, with no bank support and no one to help us if anything went wrong, it felt good.

Mick led for the first half hour, carefully negotiating

several minor rapids where the water swirled and boiled alarmingly. Several tributaries came tumbling in from the left-hand bank. We stopped to drink the ice-cold water from one of them.

Shortly we came to a difficult section where for over one hundred yards the river dropped fifty feet or so through a series of shoots and waterfalls. The canoes bobbed up and down in an eddy as I tried to spot a line down. Wary of the stoppers lining the left side of the river, I decided to try my luck on the right. Mick watched as I paddled hard, zig-zagging my way between two enormous stoppers which almost stretched across the whole width of the river, and then carefully picked a line through one hundred yards of rocks, breaking waves and smaller tricky stoppers. The rapid ended in an enormous fifty-foot diameter whirlpool and I braced hard as I almost capsized in its periphery and began circling. On the Colorado in the States I had seen giant inflatable caterpillar rafts, thirty feet long, sucked into whirlpools like this. Summoning my last reserves of energy, I broke away from the circling waters and sought haven in a placid eddy by the river bank. I waved Mick down.

He followed my line, weaving a perfect course through the water and rock hazards until at the bottom of the fall, he ploughed into the whirlpool. I watched fascinated as he spun in ever decreasing circles drawn closer to the centre where the river disappeared like the water down a plug-hole. Suddenly he was caught up in the vortex in the middle and in a split second Mick and the canoe disappeared. I sat there, completely helpless and unable to offer any aid. It must have been over a minute before I caught sight of red fibre-glass and Mick reappeared at the edge of the whirlpool and, semi-submerged, was swept downstream. He looked a comical sight as I helped him to the bank with his spraysheet ripped off, the canoe half under water, glasses askew and gasping in short gurgling breaths.

'You know,' I called back as I dragged him on the stern of my canoe, 'you don't half look a funny sight.'

'I don't know why you're laughing,' he hissed, 'because

£400 of your cameras have just gone to the bottom of the river.'

The air was blue for several minutes as I helped Mick empty his canoe out and repaired a split in the seam where the pressure in the whirlpool had forced the hull and deck apart.

We pushed on, and only then did I realise how narrowly we had averted a potentially disastrous situation, since it would have been all too easy for the canoe and Mick to have been trapped in the whirlpool. Even if Mick had managed to swim out without his canoe, there would have been little chance of rescuing the swamped boat from the swirling waters, leaving Mick with a long and arduous walk back to Kathmandu.

Pushing on, cautiously surveying each rapid as we came to it, we were anxious to avoid any further accidents.

By five pm the sun had disappeared behind a bank of cloud and a cool wind was blowing up the gorge. Pulling over to the left-hand bank, we beached the canoes and hauled them above the water line, where we found a rocky ledge to spread soaking gear out to dry.

Mick opened two cans of sardines which we devoured ravenously with our fingers. A plastic mug was retrieved from the depths of one of the canoes and, ladling a mugful of water from the river, Mick mixed up some Rise 'n Shine, agitating the water with a small stick as he tried to get the orange crystals to dissolve in the cold water. Mug after mug of river water was collected, mixed up and rapidly drunk, as we tried to slake our thirst.

Whilst Mick wrote up his diary, I stripped the sole surviving camera and patiently dried out the mechanism and lens elements. All Mick's gear was soaked, including his sleeping bag and as the shadows crept into the Dudh Kosi gorge we turned in, and tired and exhausted fell into a deep sleep.

I woke up and glanced at my watch; it said ten pm although it felt more like the early hours of the morning. I gazed up at a brilliant star-studded sky as the river lapped gently against the shore line and pondered the day ahead. We had made good time today and with luck would make the confluence by the following evening. I had agreed with Leo to wait there for three days, which would give him a breathing space to organise a helicopter to airlift us back to Kathmandu. With only one of the two helicopters operating and that already heavily booked, we rated the chances of being picked up as slim. It left us with two alternatives: to walk 150 miles back to Kathmandu or carry on canoeing down the Sun Kosi for another 500 miles until we came out into civilisation. Neither of the alternatives appealed to me and we would just have to play it by ear. It started drizzling so I slid beneath my plastic bivvy sheet determined to get some sleep. Mick, unconcerned, slept on.

I tossed and turned until sunrise and it was six am before the pale red streaks of dawn appeared on the distant horizon. I shook Mick awake who despite a soaking wet sleeping bag had slept soundly for almost twelve hours, reinforcing the manufacturer's claims that the bags were 'warm even when wet'. We crawled out of our sleeping bags, easing aching and stiff joints into protesting movement.

Mick levered open a can of fish and, isolated in the middle of Nepal, 7,000 miles from England, we savoured the delights of Aberdeen kippers and some soggy oatcake biscuits which Mick had found in the pocket of his canoeing anorak.

The whole countryside was waking up and coming alive. High on the valley side smoke was lazily curling its way up into the sky from a Sherpa dwelling and away in the distance a cow was bellowing.

Loading the boats as the shadows receded and the sun crept into the valley, we slid them into the water. The river had dropped several inches and we drifted downstream, aware that the rapids we had seen on our flight the previous day would be even more treacherous with jagged rocks, exposed, threatening to rip into our frail, millimetre-thin fibre-glass hulls. Things went well for the next four hours and at midday we found ourselves opposite a small village on the left-hand bank. I signalled to Mick to pull out and we crossed the river and landed on a shingle beach. A group of dirty, inquisitive children stood gawping and ran

149

along behind us as we crunched up the gravel and scaled a retaining wall to gain access to the village.

A fresh-faced boy ushered us into the largest of the huts, where a woman was seated in the centre and, oblivious to everything, was breast feeding a baby.

Beckoned towards a low wooden trestle, we sat down whilst a smouldering wood fire was coaxed into life. Before long a kettle was boiling away and two aluminium bowls of *tsampa* were placed in front of us. Watched by what seemed like the whole village, we tucked in until we could eat no more.

Using sign language and isolated words of Nepalese we had picked up, we tried to carry on a conversation. Where were we going to? Where had we come from? were some of the questions we were asked and we did our best to explain what we were doing. I couldn't help feeling as we left that very little had got through and they just regarded us as another bunch of 'mad Englishmen'.

We headed back to the boats and seal launched off the beach, with half a dozen children laughing and shouting to one another as the canoes gathered speed and splashed into the water. I checked the map and decided that the village we were at was no more than eight miles above the confluence and recalled from the flight in, that the section we were about to enter had been in a narrow gorge. Tracing the contours, I found the point where they ran together and located the village. A rough estimate put our position half a mile above the start of the gorge.

Soon the gleaming coloured bow of the canoe was ripping through the water as we headed downstream. Within a few minutes we found ourselves in a steeply-cut section, where the river narrowed and was channelled between soaring vertical cliffs. I drifted with the current and watched two monkeys as they playfully swung on a horizontal branch directly overhead. Suddenly they let loose with a whole fusillade of small rocks aimed at the canoes and I hastily paddled out of range, as the rocks pocketed the water around the boats.

Compressed by the vertical rock walls the river swirled and eddied, forming enormous whirlpools, surging unpredictably, giving stoppers and waves which disappeared as quickly as they formed. It made for difficult canoeing. Mick led down through the first section of gorge, expertly picking a line to avoid the worst of the water hazards.

At one point the river disappeared into a ninety-degree turn to the left. The constant erosion of the river had created a huge cavern in the right-hand wall, with dagger-like shafts of rock hanging forty feet above our heads. The backwash was enormous, with waves resounding off both walls and throwing the canoes around like corks in a wild and boiling sea. I led through the turbulent water, with Mick following closely. We emerged unscathed after two hundred yards of sustained and furious paddling.

Shortly afterwards we found a small, sunlit cove and rested for a few minutes. Anxious to make the confluence, we pushed on through progressively easier rapids. No longer were we fighting for survival on each one, but enjoying the challenge and feeling in control of the situation we shot through grade four to five rapids.

At three pm we came out of the shadows and into the sun, as we left the narrow gorge of the Dudh Kosi and paddled into the Sun Kosi.

'We've done it!' Mick yelled out excitedly. Elated with success, he came up alongside my canoe and we covered the last few yards of the Dudh Kosi together. Our euphoria was short-lived as we hit an enormous series of whirlpools swinging away down the Sun Kosi. We paddled hard and skirted around them to cross the fast-flowing current of the Sun Kosi to a sandy beach opposite the point where the two rivers merged. We ran the canoes on to the shore, clambered out and shook hands. We had made it.

Reality finally returned and we started taking note of our surroundings. The beach we had landed on was over one hundred yards long and fifty yards across at its widest point and, as Mick aptly said, with a few beer parlours, ice-cream salesmen and deck chairs it would look just like Blackpool on a summer's day. The golden sand sparkled and waves lapped against the shore where a line of flotsam and jetsam, several feet above the water level, gave some indication of how high the river had been at the peak of the monsoon.

There was little chance of climbing up the steep slabs out of the gorge.

The brightly-coloured canoes were resting on the edge of the beach, where a large overhanging rock offered some shade from the glare of the sun, as we took stock of our position. We had no food left and only half a packet of Rise 'n Shine.

'Well, what do you think, Mick?' I asked.

'You know,' he said, 'I reckon the chances of Leo getting a helicopter are pretty slim. We'll give him two days and if he's not here by then, we'll set off canoeing or walking.'

I agreed and the seriousness of our position became apparent. Without food and guides through sparsely inhabited country, the 150-mile walk would be an extremely hazardous enterprise. The alternative was to carry on canoeing and five hundred miles later meet up with the Ganges and come out into civilisation. With little idea of what lay ahead but certain of there being more formidable rapids further down the Sun Kosi gorge, and with canoes that were rapidly breaking up, this too seemed a desperate measure.

Putting these fears to the back of my mind I collected some water from the river and mixed up our last half packet of Rise 'n Shine. It barely wetted our parched throats.

Mick thought he could see a hut high on the valley wall and we decided to climb there the following day and try to obtain some food. Meanwhile an iridescent sun was sinking rapidly, illuminating the warm changing evening sky of the dying day, merging its colours into an appropriate warm coppery restful tone. Momentarily the sun hung suspended over the valley before dropping behind the sweeping ridges of the Sun Kosi.

Sleeping bags were laid out on the sand and we settled down for the night. My mind was in turmoil and I stared up at the stars winking from an inky black sky. In lonely places there is great inspiration in the sky and the stars. Our nights sleeping out on the Dudh Kosi had been relatively comfortable and I snuggled down inside my sleeping bag.

How different it all was, as I recalled the twelve nights we had spent sleeping out on the Blue Nile. Every night we had been soaked to the skin by torrential monsoon rain and in constant fear of bandit attack, had taken it in turn to wait with revolver at the ready, staring into the inky darkness. I chuckled to myself quietly as I remembered how one night when Mick and I were alone, I had suddenly woken up convinced we were surrounded by bandits. Mick, whose turn it was to guard, had fallen asleep and I nudged him awake and convinced him an attack was imminent. Revolvers were loaded and sitting back to back in our sleeping bags, each with a fistful of bullets ready to reload as soon as the magazine was empty, we waited. And we waited and waited and the following morning when we woke up the guns were still loaded and mine was pointed at Mick's head and his at mine! We finally decided that the noises we had heard were crickets in the grass. In the dark the mind plays tricks and we imagined every whistle or noise was one bandit signalling to the next. Our fears however of bandit attack were justified and four days later we did face an ambush, this time for real.

At last sleep overcame me and I slept soundly until dawn broke. Cold and anaemic heavy cotton wool clouds scudded overhead and a strong hot breeze was blowing as I wandered to the river bank, stripped off and washed in the gravelly water. Mick was awake and we started planning the day ahead.

There was a landing-strip to be marked out, food to be searched for and canoes repaired to enable us to carry on downstream if the airlift failed to materialise. We had two days to kill. Whilst I marked the landing strip out, Mick repaired the canoes. By nine am we were finished and decided to leave our trip to the native hut until the afternoon. We flopped down on top of our sleeping bags and Mick pulled out two paperbacks he had stuffed into his plastic bag as an afterthought. Mick chose to read an Alistair MacLean novel and I picked up Hamish MacInnes's story of a climb up Mount Roraima in South America. I was soon immersed in a completely different world of equatorial jungle and giant spiders. We lazed the morning away, relaxing and enjoying our total isolation from the world.

At one point a group of monkeys appeared on the

opposite cliff face and I put my book down and snapped a few shots of them as they swung across vertical slabs.

I dozed off to be suddenly awakened by a muffled banging and clattering. 'It's those bloody monkeys again,' I thought to myself and rolled over, remembering how the previous day they had thrown rocks at us. I was suddenly startled as the noise got louder and louder.

'Ye Gods! They're throwing boulders on me now, they're trying to kill me.' I quickly sat up and searched around for the culprits. There was no sign of them and as I looked up the valley there was a flash of sun against metal in the sky.

'The helicopter, it's here!' I yelled out and leapt up to grab a paddle and race out into the centre of the beach. The chopper clattered up the gorge, hovered ten feet or so above our sand bank and slowly settled, the downdraught from the rotors raising a tremendous duststorm. There were Leo and Mick Reynolds, with a pilot and engineer.

Leo and Mick ducked out beneath the rotors and came running across.

'Told you we'd do it, lads,' Leo said cheerfully, 'when we told them you'd already set off and the only way we were going to get you out of this was by helicopter, they just had to give in and find a time slot for us!'

Leo wanted to film us coming into the confluence and so whilst he got the cameras ready, we quickly changed into canoeing gear and headed back up the last two hundred yards of river. It was hard going, dodging from one eddy to the next as we avoided the worst of the water hazards and worked our way upstream.

At last we heard the whirring of the rotors and the helicopter appeared. We headed downstream the helicopter gyrating overhead and Leo filming through the side door.

Reaching the riverside at the confluence, the canoes shot into the shallows, grinding on to the golden sand; we jumped out. The cameras demanded that we shook hands and congratulated each other.

'Well, that's it!' Relief and rejoicing that was for us. Then the helicopter landed and the indefatigable Leo came dashing across.

'It's no good, lads, I just didn't get the angle right there.'

In exasperation we swore mighty futile oaths. Recognising the necessity, we then spent another half an hour fighting our way back upstream.

This time all went well and Leo got his angles right. The descent of the Dudh Kosi was finished.

The pilot discovered that with the extra weight of two passengers he now had too much fuel on board. Eight five-gallon cans of kerosene were off-loaded. A Nepalese bystander insisted on filling his paraffin lamp with some of it. Retreating, we clambered into the helicopter. The Perspex dome acted as a greenhouse and it was stifling hot. The rotors turned in the air, throwing up gigantic clouds of sand and we slowly lifted off. The young clean-shaven Nepalese pilot adjusted the trim with his left hand, carefully balancing the rotors as we rapidly gained height and forward momentum.

'You guys had a good time?' asked the pilot over his shoulder.

'You bet!' I replied.

I gazed back up the Dudh Kosi valley and it slipped to starboard, becoming a silver streak in the distance. In an hour we would be back in Kathmandu.

12

Success

KATHMANDU AIRPORT WAS A welcome sight. By 1300 hours the rotor noise was fading away and we had landed and tumbled out of the chopper and walked across the apron to the customs shed. A cheerful airport officer waved us through and we stepped into the arrivals' lounge, where John Gosling was waiting. The Transit was parked outside. Leaving Leo and Mick Reynolds to book in their camera gear for the flight back to England, we climbed into the Transit and with Gosling at the wheel, sped along the pot-holed airport perimeter road to Kathmandu.

It was a tremendous relief to be back and to have finished a descent which at times had taken on almost nightmare proportions. I was slightly saddened by the fact that those people who had put so much into the expedition, particularly Rob Hastings, had not been able to share those last few exciting days on the river, particularly that euphoric moment as we finally paddled into the Sun Kosi. However, there was little time for reflection as the Transit squealed to a halt. The Hotel Asia looked clean and inviting. I dived into a steaming hot shower to wash away the grime and filth accumulated over three days. I had lost over one and a half stone in weight and looked lean and thin in the mirror, with ribs sticking out of my chest at an alarming angle. A clean set of clothes, and then a gigantic meal of steak and chips, followed by apple pie, ice cream and fresh percolated coffee, until at last we had satisfied our ravenous hunger.

We related our adventures: Mick sinking in the whirl-pool, the monkeys throwing rocks at me, our elation and excitement when we reached the confluence, tempered by the thoughts of how we were going to get back to Kathmandu, and relief when the helicopter appeared. There was little time to waste. We planned to leave for

England the next day. It was not going to be an easy journey home, with only three drivers on the 7,400 miles return trip. Already the snows would be settling on the high Turkish passes and by the end of October they would become impassable, involving us in considerable detour and delay if we failed to get through before then. The Transit was still awaiting repairs, with the starter motor burnt out and the injection pump in need of attention. But there was no time to get them mended now. We would just have to drive back with these parts not working. Of course there was the inevitable administration to be dealt with, paperwork cleared up, bills settled, press releases written and the story told to the media.

Outside in the street, I flagged down a rickshaw and clambered aboard. Setting off in a cacophony of sound, the chain clattered, the wheels creaked and the pedals groaned as we headed down town to meet Liz Hawley, the Reuters press agent.

Driving through the busy, colourful bazaars, I noticed how much Kathmandu had changed since we arrived two months previously. The streets were thronged with Europeans and dollar-rich American tourists, armed with wads of rupee notes, were hunting out bargains. The shop-keepers loved every minute of it, restocking their shelves as quickly as the Americans could empty them. I signalled the driver to stop and with a jarring and grinding of metal against metal, as the worn brake shoes bit into the tyre rim, we came to a fitful halt.

Liz Hawley, gold rimmed spectacles perched on the end of her nose, was in the office.

Pandemonium had broken loose. Two of the American team had just made it to the summit of Everest and Miss Hawley had been summoned to a press conference along with all the other press agency representatives. She already had the story from the American Embassy, who had received an unofficial radio message from Base Camp. In the ever-competitive news business, she was already putting the story out on the wires whilst maintaining the diplomacy and tact that is required in Kathmandu and attending the 'official' news conference, to hear second hand the news she already knew. By the time the other agencies got the story it would be too late and another scoop would be chalked up to Reuters' Kathmandu office.

'Hi, I see you made it,' she yelled out as she bustled from front to back office to leave her copy to go on the Telex. News travels fast and she had heard from the airport that we had been picked up from the Sun Kosi and returned safely. With the Americans on top of Everest, our own story seemed a little over-shadowed and, giving her brief details of our trip, we left her to dash off to the press conference.

A quick call at the bank, a visit to Mike Cheney and then back to the hotel to write the expedition report for Leo to take out on his flight the next day.

I finished in the early hours of the morning and once again exhausted, fell into bed.

We were away by eight am the next morning. A fine warm day it was, as we started along the Pokkhara Road, running alongside the Trisuli River. It was an excellent white water river and we peered through the windows at its rapids, until eventually we lost sight as it disappeared into a steep gorge. I remarked at the time that it would make a fine rafting river. I was to learn later that a commercial rafting concern was starting operating on it the following year.

Pokkhara has none of the tourist attractions of Kathmandu and we paused only briefly for a meal before heading up towards the Indian-Nepalese border, which we reached early the next morning. We were directed into a compound and instructed to unload the vehicle. Sweating and becoming increasingly hot tempered in the clammy heat, we unloaded and unpacked the Transit.

'There are only two canoes, where are the other ten?' asked a customs officer. 'You realise you must pay 200 per cent customs duty on anything you do not take out of Nepal.'

There followed a bitter argument and wrangling as I tried to explain how the canoes had been written off on our canoe expedition.

'Whereabouts are they?' asked the same officer.

Patiently, I explained again, this time saying they were lost canoeing down Everest. It brought hoots of laughter from the bystanders. The customs officer, deciding that I was taking him for a ride, handed me over to the police for interrogation. The wrangling continued and eventually I compromised, paid 1,000 rupees and crossed rapidly into India, before they checked through the massive inventory I had filed as I checked into Nepal and discovered other discrepancies.

Delhi was reached in two days and we spent a hectic six hours renewing visas for Afghanistan. Whilst these were being prepared Roger went shopping for cheese cloth shirts. He came back empty handed, surprised to find that although the shirts are made in India, they were twice the price he could buy them for at Bradford's John Street, market! That's one of the vagaries of international trading. With quotas and tariffs, it is often cheaper to buy the exported goods in a country 7,000 miles away, than it is to buy them on the home market.

Collecting our visas, we drove for eighteen hours to the Pakistan border. Then disaster struck, as a flashing oil warning light alerted us to a steady stream of boiling hot oil pouring from the engine. There was nothing for it but to limp the fifteen miles to Lahore, stopping frequently to refill the engine with oil.

After much searching, we found a Ford garage and the engine was inspected. The damage was worse than we expected with both camshaft and crankshaft oil seals needing replacement, in addition to a worn bearing in the diesel injection pump. This had to be removed, stripped down, new bearings pressed into place, checked over and replaced; in all, two days' work. Our enforced stop did give us a breathing space, since we had been on the go almost continuously for five days and we ate and slept the time away.

The van was finished on October 18th and we continued our drive, crossing the Kabul Pass on the 19th and heading across the scorching hot plains of Afghanistan and on into Iran. It was flat featureless country and we drove almost continuously; with no starter motor and over four tons dead-weight of van and equipment to push, we just dared not stop for fear of never getting started again!

In the early hours of the morning, we would search desperately for hills where we could park the van and snatch a few hours' sleep, without the perpetual bucketing and rolling motion which accompanied trying to sleep with the van on the move. Intensely five pairs of eyes would stare through the window as the headlights picked out the contours and relief. It frequently turned out to be an exercise which lasted several hours. Since the driver had the ultimate decision and unless he could be convinced he was on an incline, he would be reluctant to stop and put the decision to the definitive test: to fetch the vehicle to a halt, put the engine into neutral, release the brake and wait for it to roll forward. If it did, we applied the handbrake, switched the engine off and fell asleep, assured that the vehicle would roll forward and jump start the next morning.

In the dark it was extremely difficult to get a true perspective and one night, which will always stick in my memory, we were all desperately tired and hungry. Roger, who was at the wheel, took the initiative and decided to sleep. Since we were descending a hill, now was the best time. I propped myself up on my elbows and from the back seat, where I was dozing, looked through the windscreen and was convinced we were on a steep incline as the headlights picked out the surrounding landmarks.

'Oh, give it a go!' I called out. We stopped and Roger knocked the gearbox into neutral and we waited expectantly for the wheels to begin turning as he released the handbrake. To our absolute amazement the van slowly gathered speed, going backwards! Our perspective had been so far out that we were going up a steep hill and not down! Making the most of his mistake, a red-faced Roger spun the van around and we fell asleep, facing back the way we had come.

The miles flew past. Out of Iran into Turkey and by now the hot weather of Asia was beginning to deteriorate. The heater was reconnected and wipers swept the windscreen as we hit first rain and then snow. The high Turkish passes were covered in a three-inch layer of freshly-fallen, wet snow and we skidded and slid our way to the top. By law

Dave Manby breaks through a stopper.

An early morning audience for the first rapid before breakfast.

Mike Jones.

you are required to carry chains from October onwards in Turkey but with the driving snow and sleet no one was going to stop us and check.

Another breakdown. This time I was at the wheel and we were at the foot of one of the passes. I clambered out, rolled up my sleeves and tinkered around inside the engine. The metal was cold and finger-tips rapidly numbed as I tried to locate the problem. In the distance there was the rumble of heavy wagons and three giant articulated container lorries came swaying around the corner. They were English and their drivers pulled up behind.

'Having trouble, mate?' asked one of the drivers.

'Here you are, Jack'll fix it.'

A colossal toolkit was produced and within five minutes the engine was firing away. It was only a blocked fuel filter. We stood around talking for a few minutes. They told me they did the run from Bristol to Iran and back again every three weeks. Sooner them than me, I thought to myself.

At last we made Ankara and then Istanbul. We stopped briefly to buy Turkish delight, the original sweet sickly gelatinous variety that sticks to your teeth and to the roof of your mouth. Then across the Bosphorus and into Europe. Miles and kilometres of never ending roads. Retsina and ouzo in Greece, black bread and cheese in Yugoslavia, wienerschnitzel in Austria and steins of beer in Germany, where Renate Kolloch, Mick Hopkinson's girlfriend, was anxiously awaiting our return.

We relaxed and rested up for a day in Frankfurt before setting off for the reception which had been arranged for us in England. Our problems were not over and we arrived at Ostend to find that the ferry ticket was missing. Anxiously I searched for it but it had been over four months since we'd crossed the Channel and its whereabouts evaded me. I even wondered if I'd left it in Nepal as I sifted through my brief-case. Eventually it turned up and we rolled on board the ship.

A swift trip across the Channel and the ferry quickly berthed. It was the middle of a cold and cheerless night. What a welcome home! It was too late for the pubs and even the fish-and-chip shops were closed. After four months together there was a feeling of anticlimax; a mood of depression settled on the team. Driving in silence until thirty miles south of London; the irrepressible Roger then remembered the case of sparkling wine Renate had sent us on our way with and a spontaneous party developed. Even the driver joined in the alcoholic festivities, stacking the wine bottles against the door of the Transit which was all well and good, until we stopped in the centre of London to ask the way, opened the door and with a tinkle of glass six wine bottles went rolling across the road and into the gutter at the feet of a watching policeman. We beat a hasty retreat and, highly merry, found Rob Hastings' house, dragged him out of bed and continued the party. It was almost dawn.

A couple of hours' sleep and then on to Cardiff and HTV. The rush prints, a black and white copy taken off the colour negative and the movie film were ready and excitedly we watched them through on a film editor. And then back to Leo's where Barbara had been slaving over the hot stove all day, to produce a gargantuan feast. Bloated with food and wine, we came to what should have been the highlight of the day's entertainment; a special showing of Leo's TV film about a climb on the North Face of the Matterhorn. The projector was set up, screen adjusted and lights dimmed. We settled down in the living room to watch the film. No sooner had I sat down than I felt murmuring waves of sleep drifting over me and I woke up as the final few frames were fed through the projector. Bleary eyed, I looked around. Everyone was fast asleep, including Barbara, and poor old Leo, waiting for applause and praise at the end of the film had nothing but snores and grunts as everyone woke up.

Next day Bristol Street Motors had arranged a press conference in Birmingham. Luck was certainly not on our side and we made a hundred yards down the road from Leo's Bristol home when there was an ominous clunk from the engine and we ground to a halt. A call was put through to Birmingham and we adjourned to Leo's to eat the masses of food left from the previous evening, until a tow truck appeared and we made an ignominious entry to the Bristol Street showrooms, hitched up to a four-ton breakdown wagon. Fortunately the press had long abandoned our overdue return.

Bristol Street could not have done more. An almost new Ford Cortina Estate was put at my disposal and we zoomed across the city and on to the motorway, and headed north to Yorkshire and home. For everyone it was the end of the expedition; for me it was the start of another two months' work winding up the trip. There were articles to write, photos to sort through, select and caption, the TV film to be produced, sponsors to write to and thank for their help, and TV and radio interviews to give. A book was commissioned and I embarked upon a hectic lecture circuit, lecturing everywhere from London to the far north of Scotland.

Bristol Street held a full enquiry into the engine failure. They thought the problem lay with the oil we had been putting into the engine, since when it was dismantled they found the oil sludged in the sump. An immediate analysis of the oil we had been using was ordered and to our amazement, and no doubt theirs, they found that the twenty-gallon drum of so called 'engine oil' I had bought in Iran was in fact cooking oil and was excellent for frying fish and chips but no good for high velocity bearings.

In those brief exciting four months what had we achieved? We had succeeded in setting a world altitude record for canoeing at 17,500 feet and earned ourselves a place in the *Guinness Book of Records* by descending eighty miles of the highest and, without doubt, some of the most difficult and dangerous rapids in the world. We had developed and pioneered rough water techniques and standards in arduous and unfamiliar conditions, spurred on no doubt by the scepticism shown to our plan.

On a more personal level we had brought together a group of diverse individuals, each with their own motives for joining the expedition, and seen them moulded into a group where everyone forgot their own hopes, aims and ambitions and worked for the good of the expedition. No one could have asked for a better and more loyal team. Of course there were arguments and disagreements which flared up one minute and were forgotten the next, but as well as being successful we were a happy bunch.

And what of the team themselves, what did they get out of it? Over the course of the expedition they made many new friendships and strengthened old ones, had the opportunity to travel and experience different lifestyles, seeing at first hand the poverty and backwardness of India and Pakistan contrasted with the shimmering warm beauty of Nepal and the stark splendour of the mountains. But, above all, they found out a few things about themselves: they experienced disappointment and frustration, at times anger, doubts and fears, and then success and triumph, going through the spectrum of human emotions and coming out that much richer for the experience. Each person contributed his own special talents to the expedition. Leo Dickinson's imaginative camera work, Rob Hastings' practical flair, John Liddell's meticulous accounting and handling of the porters, John Gosling's culinary skills, Mick Hopkinson's brilliance in a canoe, Dave Manby who struck up a remarkable rapport with the porters, and of course Roger Huyton's cheery and indomitable sense of humour. And one mustn't forget those people on the periphery of the expedition whose contribution was so important, in particular the enthusiasm of our Nepalese staff who entered so much into the spirit of thngs, even to the extent of spectating from the bank and laughing, clapping and cheering when we capsized!

No analysis would be complete without looking at my own motivation for embarking upon those many months of back-breaking, at times disappointing and other times immensely exciting work, involved with putting an expedition on the road, taking part and then closing it down.

I gain a tremendous amount of satisfaction from conceiving, creating, expanding and finally accomplishing an expedition. I find it a fascinating experience tackling problems, coming up with solutions and developing the skills and experience to see these through to fruition. Each problem requires its own special approach, whether it be puzzling out how to mount a camera on a canoe or persuading a major sponsor to part with a large sum of money. It's time consuming and sometimes it involves the tenacity of the badger and others the finesse of the smoothest of diplomats. One meets a rich variety of people of all types and backgrounds and is uplifted by the humour, courage and reaction that one gets to the mention of their involvement in these adventurous projects. This involvement of many people in what, after all, is an adventure, is very satisfying.

'After Everest doesn't everything seem an anticlimax?' is a question which is frequently posed as I go around lecturing. Each river has its own special attractions and unique set of problems, whether it be the alligators and piranha fish of a South American river, the thrills and spills of trying to shoot the racing torrents coming off the Himalayas, or the unfriendly natives in the middle of the African jungle.

Within two days of arriving home in Yorkshire everyone was talking of where we would go next. Was it to be South America, Nepal again or perhaps the Karakoram. At the time, I felt disinclined to be associated with such a massive expedition again and accept the mental and physical strain that such an undertaking inevitably imposes. Time however mellows the thoughts of hardship and strain. Before long it is the pleasures and excitements that remain dominant, even in the recesses of the mind. Canoes flashing through the sun glinting on the cataracts of Everest, and the cold majestic peaks of the Himalayas; the Sherpa kids dancing up and down with excitement on the river banks; the young Sherpa cook nonchalantly climbing Leo's severe rock face; the relief on all our faces when Mick was recovering on the bank after his capsize; the tinkling of the prayer wheels and bells at the monasteries. This is the warm and glowing imagery of remembrance, not the cold boredom of mishaps and grinding frustration.

Before long, I was planning for expeditions to the Orinoco in South America and back to the east for the Karakoram.

Why do we do it? It is the question that is always asked. Curiosity? Challenge? No doubt there are deep psychological and philosophical answers to this question. My answer is comparatively homespun and simple. You conceive the idea, you plan it, you carry it out and you get a great feeling of satisfaction. Happiness is struggling against the huge elemental pounding waters of some strange river, being rushed, hurtled, jolted and thrown about the boat with every muscle of the body and every fibre of the mind fully stretched for survival, as one hurtles excitedly through the swirling waters, where no one has travelled before.

At the end of the day, peace, quiet, warmth, food and friendship.

APPENDIX 1

Transport

IN CHOOSING THE OVERLAND route to Nepal across Europe we opted for the cheapest and most economical way of transporting personnel and the mass of equipment we had assembled to Kathmandu. It was, however, subject to delay and hold-ups at border crossings, the vagaries of the weather and the inevitable risk of breakdown.

We were fortunate in enlisting the support of Bristol Street Motors Ltd, and they supplied, at no cost to the expedition, a brand-new, fifteen-seater Ford Diesel Transit. It was equipped to Ford specifications with heavy duty suspension and electrical system, sump guards, and even cloth seats and stereo system. A tachometer was fitted to comply with EEC regulations and the firm of W. Thomas from West Bromwich was given the job of designing and producing a roof carrier. A comprehensive kit of spares and workshop manual came with the vehicle.

The Overseas Branch of the Automobile Association provided route details and travel documentation, including a Carnet for the Transit. This is a series of counterfoiled forms in which details of the vehicle are recorded as it enters and leaves each country. The Carnet is a guarantee from the AA to pay customs duty should the vehicle by reason of accident, theft or sale fail to leave the country. They, in turn, expect to be indemnified against the risk of this happening, which requires either a letter from the bank guaranteeing the highest duty payable, in our case £10,000, or the risk can be minimised by taking out insurance. In our case the premium would have been in the region of £500. Fortunately Bristol Street Motors Finance Department provided the necessary letter of guarantee. EEC documents in the form of Motor Vehicle Passenger Waybill and drivers' log books were supplied through the local branch of the Road Transport Authority.

The financial side was closely monitored. A petrol and oil logbook was kept in which prices and mileages at fill-ups were recorded. This enabled us to keep check on the fuel consumption as well as produce accounts at the end of the trip. John Liddell's calculator was worth its weight in gold, checking on petrol prices and doing the inevitable trans-actions between currencies which are involved in crossing ten separate countries.

And then for the emergencies. A good rope and hydraulic jack for lifting and pulling the vehicle out of trouble are essential. We had a tow bar fitted to the rear and a bolt hitch to the front. Unfortunately the latter was ripped out of its mountings at our first major break-down, when the tow vehicle set off like a dragster. Floodwater is a common problem and our Diesel Transit with no electrics survived several immersions without any serious consequences. The technique of negotiating a severely flooded road is worth mentioning. A bow wave is built up in front of the vehicle by moving slowly into the water, keeping the engine revs high and slipping the clutch. Using this method, the vehicle can negotiate deep water, pushing a wall of water in front of it. In a petrol engine, it is necessary to disconnect the fan belt to stop water being sprayed over the electrical system. And, of course, when the vehicle comes out of the water, it is necessary to run for a short time with the vehicle in low gear and the foot on the brake to dry out brake shoes. The first time, we forgot this with almost disastrous con-sequences.

And finally, creature comforts. Air conditioning would be the ultimate in luxury. We had to make do with an ice box and a plentiful supply of beer and Coca-Cola. Sweets broke the boredom and we had a boxful of paperbacks given by Pan Books to while away the hours on the road. Delays were mainly at border crossings. A list of names of passen-gers, passport numbers, places of issue, date of expiry saved time and endless paperwork and of course delay in crossing from one border to the next.

Inevitably some spare parts cannot be carried and they

are the ones which are frequently required. There are two alternatives if this situation should arise. Sometimes it is possible to buy used parts or copied parts made up locally. This applies in particular to vehicles such as Volkswagen, Land Rovers, Bedford trucks and Ford wagons which are seen and used extensively in Asia. It is a worthwhile exercise to check with the manufacturer which countries they export your particular vehicle to, and obtaining location of the importers, since in the event of a serious break-down, this may be the only place which can put you back on the road.

Where all possible avenues have been exhausted for obtaining spare parts, the only recourse is to get them from England. Our own experience taught us that for this to work successfully and quickly, it is essential to have a contact in England, preferably a garage who can obtain parts speedily and have them air cargoed out.

Several things were missed from the Transit in our initial planning. Calibrated oil and temperature gauges are essential. When the temperature gauge reaches the red zone it is frequently too late and the same applies to a flashing oil warning light. With known operating temperature and pressures, the performance of the engine can be closely monitored.

A good set of spotlights are essential and not a luxury. Travelling in the darkness, although much cooler, is frequently hazardous with unlit bullock carts, trailers, wagons and people on the road. For the same reason a substantial klaxon, even a ship's hooter, would not go amiss; to clear people from the road is essential. Long-range fuel tanks and a filter on the petrol tank intake considerably extend the distance between fill-ups, and remove the nagging doubts that you are going to run out in the middle of the desert; they also enable you to fill up in the cheap countries and avoid buying petrol in the more expensive. We made do with jerry cans which is both messy and time-consuming, as well as posing an appreciable fire risk.

The expedition was responsible for vehicle insurance and this was taken out through Derek Brown Insurances Ltd, a subsidiary of Bristol Street Motors. Fully comprehensive insurance with Green Card cover for three months was £100 with a £250 excess. Derek Brown, who act as insurance brokers, were unable to find anyone to insure us past Istanbul, not even third party. This problem is not unusual and it is normal practice, and in most countries compulsory, to purchase third party insurance at border crossings, to cover transit time across the country. Fully comprehensive cover is available in Iran and India, but tends to be expensive.

AA Five Cover was considered but not taken out, which was a mistake, since the comprehensive service it offers across Europe with part location, delivery and vehicle recovery, would be well worthwhile.

A group expedition policy was taken out with a local Bradford broking firm to cover the contents of the van and other valuable items of expedition equipment.

The problems we experienced on the overland journey have already been catalogued. It is essential to have someone in charge of routine vehicle maintenance and Rob Hastings took on this job, checking water, oil and battery levels daily, inspecting tyres for uneven wear, taking pressures, and looking around the vehicle for any tell-tale oil leaks. A few minutes each morning can possibly save a catastrophic break-down.

On the spares side, we found we were short of certain items which with foresight and more careful planning could have been avoided. We hadn't realised that the timing mechanism was a belt drive and consequently had not got a spare when it broke. And something which should be checked very carefully on modern-day engines, with more than one fan belt driving accessories such as servo and air-conditioners, is the size of the belts, since they frequently differ and, as we found to our cost, a spare belt for one would not fit the other.

Acknowledgments:
Airstream, Bristol Street Motors, Derek Brown Insurance and W. Thomas.

APPENDIX 2

Equipment

THE REACTION OF EQUIPMENT manufacturers and suppliers to my requests for help and assistance brought a varied response. Many entered enthusiastically into the spirit of things and provided goods at no cost to the expedition or at greatly reduced rates. Production schedules were fitted around our requirements, consignments diverted en route to customers and special deliveries laid on to get equipment to us on time.

For canoeing equipment, I went for tried and tested items, and manufacturers whom I knew could produce a product which would stand up to the high degree of usage and rigorous conditions which we would meet in the Himalayas.

I asked Graham Mackereth of Pyranha Mouldings to design a canoe for the descent, with the only parameters that it should be a high volume boat and weigh no more than thirty pounds. On heavy water, a high volume design has enough buoyancy to ride well above the water, shed waves quickly, and if lightweight, is very manoeuvrable. The Everest Elite, designed over a two-month period, fulfilled these criteria and was universally liked by the expedition paddlers.

It was constructed as follows using polyester resin. The hull was made of two layers of 1 oz glass mat and one layer of 10 oz per square metre polyester fabric. Reinforcing patches of Kevlar in plain weave at 7 oz per square yard were positioned under the seat at bow and stern.

A longitudinal wood strengthener, covered in two layers of 1½ oz glass mat, ran along the centre of the hull.

The deck was made up of two layers of 1 oz glass mat with 10 oz per square metre polyester fabric from bow to feet area and from the rear of the cockpit to stern. An additional layer of 1½ oz glass mat was placed around the cockpit and a longitudinal strengthener covered by two layers of 1½ oz glass mat, and seven transverse herringbone strengtheners in 2 oz glass mat, completed the deck.

Hull and deck were seamed both inside and out, as opposed to the normal practice of joining hull and deck by a single inside seam. Experience was to prove that the extra strength from the double seams was essential.

Adjustable footrests were fitted, as the canoes were to be used by different individuals, each with varying leg lengths. My own preference is for a more solid aluminium bar fibre-glassed in position but where people are continually changing canoes this proved impractical.

Buoyancy in the form of rigid expanded polystyrene blocks were fibre-glassed in position. We would have been well advised to pack all the canoes with extra buoyancy to reduce damage when swamped and help retrieval from the river.

Only six of the twelve canoes were fitted with camera mountings. This almost proved a disaster, as three of the camera boats were lost in the early stages of the expedition. Ideally, all the canoes should have camera mountings on future trips.

Himalayan rivers are expensive on canoes and out of the twelve Everest Elite canoes we transported to Nepal, only three were intact at the end of the trip, the remainder having been lost downstream or broken up against rocks.

A comprehensive fibre-glass repair kit supplied by Pyranha Mouldings was used sporadically, most people preferring to mend the canoes using a PVC tape supplied by the 3Ms Company or a cloth-backed one from Warrior Tapes.

Paddles came from a variety of sources. Alistair Wilson supplied Lendal fibre-glass-shafted white water blades, which were used mostly by myself and occasionally by the other team members. I prefer these because of their lightness to the heavier Prijon blades which were the mainstay of the expedition. Everyone used right-hand feather blades, and 215 cm seemed to be the most popular length. The longer the paddle, the more leverage it is possible to achieve, for example when climbing out of a stopper or eskimo rolling, and on rough water at 215 cm would seem to be a compromise between a short compact slalom paddle of say 210 cm and a long unwieldy white water racing 220 cm length.

We all taped around the blade area with PVC tape. Should the blade break on a rapid, the tape is sufficient to hold the broken pieces together and allow the paddler to reach the bank.

In all, twenty paddles were taken but only one was broken and one lost downriver. My own opinion would be that we escaped lightly, and I fully expected to break or lose half our. paddles, and had taken several spare four-foot aluminium tubes into which the blades can be slotted if they are broken across the shaft and used in an emergency.

Neoprene spraydecks were supplied at cost by Typhoon of London. They performed well and were watertight even in the heaviest water.

Robin Witter of Ace Canoe Products, Chester, supplied crash helmets. Robin is a colourful character in the canoeing world and puts the same amount of energy into his plastics business as he did into canoeing eight years ago, when he was in the British team. He produces a first-rate product that is light, comfortable and smart to wear. In three separate incidents the helmets saved team members from serious head injury when they were dashed against the boulders that littered the river bed.

Lifejackets were supplied by the Manchester-based firm of Harishok, run by the enterprising Calverley family. They were well made, and the component closed cell foam, which made up the filling of the jackets, survived the hard wear and tear to which it was subjected.

I am often asked why in those extreme conditions we failed to wear full wetsuits. The absence of wetsuits was caused, no doubt, by my own dislike of wearing them and my lack of drive to find a company to sponsor them. Wetsuit trousers were, however, in evidence much of the time and saved Mick Hopkinson and Roger Huyton from more severe injury as they were dashed against rocks on their swims downriver.

As a top cover Damart Thermawear Double Force vests were worn. Apart from being extremely warm, they dry rapidly; essential when no drying facilities are available.

Canoe cagoules were worn on top of the Damart, and these again were provided by Harishok. The Velcro neck fastenings and neoprene wrist bands successfully prevented water getting into inner clothing in all but the most extreme conditions.

Footwear varied from wetsuit bootees, Adidas training shoes to a pair of shiny black dress shoes which Dave Manby insisted on wearing.

Various items of equipment, including cameras, were carried in the canoes. Harishok provided plastic heat welded bags with a watertight closing. The seams tended to rip apart and we opted for the more reliable BDH screwtop cannisters or heavy duty plastic fertiliser bags,which, if used correctly, are a hundred per cent waterproof.

Since we were going no higher than 18,000 feet, camping and walking gear came off the shelf.

Bob Brigham of Ellis Brighams Ltd supplied tentage, stoves, Lilo airbeds, head torches, cooking pots and pans, knife and fork sets and an ample supply of water sterilising tablets.

The tentage consisted of six Vango Force 10 Mark IVs and one Vango frame tent. Of the Force 10 tents, four were lightweight and two were standard. They performed faultlessly in the torrential monsoon rain, apart from some problems with the heat-sealed seams which were easily ripped by rough handling, and plastic groundsheets, several of which suffered holes caused by candles or cigarettes burning through them.

Most of the cooking in Nepal was on wood fires but on the overland journey the Optimus petrol stoves were invaluable for numerous roadside 'brew-ups' and meals. Our experience was to prove that petrol stoves are particularly to be recommended because of the difficulties in obtaining paraffin.

Karrimor products were used extensively. The ever-popular Karrimats were used as insulation at night and, as many walkers and climbers have found, they were invaluable for a comfortable night's sleep.

Totem Senior rucksacks used in conjunction with K2 pack frames were used by all the members of the expedition. They were spacious, carried well and, true to the reputation Karrimor have built up over the years, performed faultlessly through the course of the expedition. Very popular Karrimor products were the ski packs which were worn around the waist and the pouch performed a multitude of invaluable tasks, as a purse, moneybelt, first-aid kit, camera case, battery-holder for TV cameras and a variety of other important functions.

Peter Hutchison of Mountain Equipment provided sleeping bags. They were square-toed, synthetic pile-filled and had full-length zips. They were versatile, being light and yet warm right up to 18,000 feet. Drying out rapidly if accidentally soaked, and as Mick Hopkinson proved, 'warm even when wet' by spending a comfortable night in a bag that had been retrieved from a swamped canoe.

YHA Services of Birmingham provided at cost, walking boots. Various types were used, principally Scarpa and Pinnacle brands, and after the initial breaking-in period, these proved to be comfortable and sturdy enough to withstand the continual soaking they were subjected to. Laces fared badly and several pairs are essential for anyone contemplating a similar expedition.

Walking clothing consisted of Damart shirts, some extremely smart and stylish sweaters provided by Pringle of Scotland and a variety of shorts and walking breeches. Umbrellas purchased locally in Kathmandu were used as sun shades in the morning and for their intended purpose in the afternoons when the monsoon rains came.

At higher altitudes, intense reflection from the snow was a problem and a variety or sun creams were used. Extremely effective sun glasses were given by the British-American Optical Company and these were used around Base Camp.

For cold and wet weather we had cag-jacs supplied by G and H Products from Batley and Grenfell jackets supplied by Grenfell. Both were much in evidence the higher we went and wore extremely well.

Carrying things and keeping them dry on the walk in is always a problem and we tried a variety of containers.

Warwick Production Company supplied six extremely versatile aluminium chests with snap fastenings and waterproof lids. They were used almost exclusively for carrying camera equipment and film, and in this respect were successful. The Metal Box Company supplied over forty two-feet cubed biscuit tins, which were a cheap and effective method of storing, carrying and keeping equipment and food dry.

A variety of plastic bags were taken, supplied by Bakelite-Xylonite and Transatlantic Plastics. The ever-popular orange sheeting used by the porters to shield them from the rain was supplied by Storey's of Lancaster.

Office equipment in the form of a miniature note-taking machine and a larger portable battery cassette recorder, were supplied by Philips Electrical. Blank tapes were supplied by BASF and pre-recorded ones by Phonogram.

Crockery was supplied by Antiference from their Melaware range and their Big Daddy mugs proved extremely popular, which accounted in part to the vast amount of tea we drank, since they hold over one pint each!

Spear and Jackson of Sheffield provided a variety of saws which were invaluable for cutting branches and logs for the kitchen fires.

Acknowledgments:
Adidas, Ace Canoe Products, Acme Whistles, Antiference, Bakelite Xylonite, BASF United Kingdom, Brighams, British American Optical Co, Damart, Fibo, G and H Products, Grenfell, Harishok, Haythorne Thwaite and Sons, Insulpak, Karrimor International, Lendal Products, Macpherson Train Co, Metal Box Co, Minnesota Manufacturing and Mining Co, Mountain Equipment, Pan Books, PGL, Philips, P and H Fibreglass Products, Phonogram, Pyranha Mouldings, Pringle, Pye Telecommunications, E T Skinner, Spear and Jackson, Storey's, Transatlantic Plastics, Triwall Containers, Warrior Tapes, Warwick Production Company and the Youth Hostels Association.

APPENDIX 3

Photography

WITH TWO PROFESSIONAL PHOTOGRAPHERS accompanying the expedition and several keen amateur ones there was no excuse for not obtaining full photographic coverage of the entire expedition.

Leo Dickinson with Mick Reynolds from HTV Cardiff as an additional cameraman, took charge of shooting the professional 16 mm TV film, and in all 12,000 feet of Kodak Eastman Colour Negative film with a running time of approximately five and half hours was shot. This was edited to a fifty-two minute documentary and screened by HTV on the commercial network and is being shown all over the world.

The camera equipment was as follows:
1. Arriflex ST + 3 prime lenses and Angenieux 12–120 mm
2. Beaulieu R 16 + Canon Macro Florite 12–120 mm
3. Canon Scopic with 12.5–76 mm lens
4. Bell & Howell DR 70 + three prime lenses
5. Bell & Howell Autoload with 6 mm Canon VTR lens
6. Bell & Howell Electroload (modified to electric drive) and 6 mm lens.

No sound equipment was taken and the film track was dubbed on in the labs.

Two underwater housings constructed by Harry Horton of Aquasnap, Bridgwater, were used. One was for the Canon Scopic, and the other took the modified Autoload and was bolted to the canoes.

Problems were experienced by the camera team in keeping up with the canoeists on the extremely fast water.

Several hours spent tramping through dense undergrowth to a camera position was sometimes rewarded by a few seconds of film as the canoes flashed past.

It was fortunate that Leo Dickinson, together with Geoff Tabbner and Eric Jones who acted as camera assistants, were all experienced climbers, since at several points it was necessary to climb into the gorge to film canoe sequences.

The most successful and visually exciting film was taken from the canoes themselves on the modified Bell & Howell and 16 mm VTR lens. Using one of several positions on the canoes, it was possible to give the TV viewer at first hand the view the canoeist has as he descends the rapids. In total, twenty fifty-foot cassettes were shot off on the canoes, with one-third running at 75 fps to give a slow motion effect.

Sixteen millimetre coverage of training in Austria and the overland journey used in newscasts by the BBC and ITN was taken by Mike Jones on reversal Kodak 7242 stock, using a Bell & Howell 70 DR.

Amateur cine coverage was achieved using a Bell & Howell 1218 Super 8 movie camera. The camera was used by one of several operators and, considering their inexperience, the results were surprisingly good. Three and a half hours of film was shot and this was spliced together into a half hour film of the descent, and used in subsequent lectures and talks where the movie film was found to be more effective than static 35 mm slides.

On the stills side, over one hundred reels of 36-exposure Kodachrome 25 film were shot off. Canon equipment was much in evidence and Leo's Canon F1 with MF motor drive and selection of lenses from 20 mm to 300 mm bagged the best shots.

Mike Jones carried a Nikkonas underwater camera with 35 mm lens and this was used for limited coverage by the canoeists whilst they were on the water.

The remainder of the team used a variety of cameras, and achieved reasonable results.

Whilst for many people the expedition was over once we got back to England, Leo Dickinson spent many weeks mounting, sorting through and cataloguing our vast slide collection, and together with Terry Elgar from HTV, editing and producing the 16 mm TV film which portrays all the facets of the expedition and is a credit to Leo's artistic talent.

So far, this brilliant film has picked up the following awards:

April 1978 The Gold Gentian, Italian Alpine Club Award, Trento, Italy, International Film Festival.

May 1978 Grand Prix, 7th International Festival of Sports Films, Paris.

Sept 1978 Diable d'Or Prize, Prix du Public, 9th International Festival of Mountaineering Films, Diablerets, Switzerland.

Acknowledgments:
Aquasnap, Bell & Howell, Canon, HTV Cardiff, Kodak, Nikkon, *Observer* Magazine and Rank Audio Visual.

APPENDIX 4

Catering

THIS WAS A MASSIVE undertaking. In all, some 184 letters were individually typed to food companies, manufacturers and suppliers requesting sponsorship. Sixty replied saying they were unable to help, eighty offered their products free or at discount rates, and around forty never replied at all. The total cost of products obtained was £1,900, and the approximate cost of obtaining these was £200.

Inevitably organising the food was left until the last minute. A massive list was drawn up of possible sponsors, using addresses taken off tins and packets in a local supermarket, and contacts John Gosling had built up as a catering manager.

Letters were despatched and the following week John began the mammoth task of chasing each letter up individually. The system was not infallible. A letter was mistakenly sent to Nabisco asking for Weetabix. They pointed out that Weetabix was their main competitor in the breakfast cereal market, but sportingly offered to supply their shredded wheat product! Another startled biscuit manufacturer who regularly supports expeditions rang up to query the date: did we really intend leaving in less than three weeks or was it 1977 we were setting off?

Whilst John was busy organising quantities and deliveries, I began scrutinising catering reports of climbing expeditions to the Himalayas.

Since we were not going higher than Base Camp Everest, it seemed highly probable that we could buy food from villages along the route. However, allowing for the worst possible eventualities, I felt we ought to plan to be totally self-sufficient, which would require enough food for eighteen men away from Kathmandu for six weeks. The eighteen men came from the thirteen-strong European contingent and five Nepalese staff, who Mike Cheney had informed me would share the same rations as ourselves.

Once away from Kathmandu, everything would have to be carried by porters through the monsoon-swept Himalayan foothills. On his Everest expeditions in 1972 and 1975 Chris Bonington had been very successful in using heavy duty waxed cardboard boxes for carrying food through to Base Camp and I contacted Anthony Welton of Triwall, who manufactured them, and he generously agreed to make forty available immediately. These were collected two days later, and when packed so that they weighed no more than sixty pounds, were ideal to carry to Base Camp.

As deliveries arrived, John Gosling made an inventory and slowly began to plan menus. If there were deficiencies, he sat down and phoned around until eventually he came up with the required ingredients or product. John has the ability to sell ice-creams to the Eskimos and when it came to buying the few things we were short of, he had been so successful that we required no more than a housewife would buy on a Saturday morning shopping trip.

As I have mentioned in Chapter 2, two days before departure a massive production line was set up at Leamington Spa and an army of girlfriends, relatives and helpers descended on a Leamington school hall to begin the mammoth task of breaking bulk ingredients down to individually wrapped portions, weighing out, labelling, packing and finally sealing into boxes. We had twenty food boxes each containing enough food for eighteen men for two days. There was everything from toilet tissue, bars of soap, to a full three-course meal. We had found that to keep within the weight limits, it was impossible to include tinned products, and dehydrated meat, vegetables and potatoes were the mainstay of our evening meal. Breakfast was a cereal, generally porridge, followed by pancakes and Ryvita biscuits. Lunch was more Ryvitas with a meat or fish spread and chocolate biscuits. Coffee, tea, Marvel and sugar with a few luxuries were included in each box.

We had enough food left over after packing twenty food boxes to keep thirteen people in food for two and a half weeks' training in Austria, eleven people fed for the month-long overland trip, and John Gosling's cat in mackerel for one and a half years!

Did we learn anything from our catering arrangements? One of the most disastrous mistakes was storing fibre-glass near food boxes and having to eat fibre-glass tainted food for over six weeks, the message was brought home very strongly to everyone in the expedition.

By and large the food was adequate, although it lacked variety and at times tended to become monotonous. We took more than ample quantities and it would have been well worthwhile sacrificing quantity and going for some tinned meat and fruit.

Luxuries were much sought after but scarce; two or three food boxes with chocolate, cakes, biscuits, sweets and Christmas puddings would have been a sound investment.

Much food can be bought locally, particularly potatoes and rice which are relatively cheap and certainly more acceptable than instant potatoes.

Had we been a smaller party, say no more than four Europeans, it would have been possible and, without doubt, cheaper to buy meals on the way and carry the minimum of food and cooking equipment for emergencies.

Acknowledgments:
Ambrosia Creamery, Ansells, Associated Biscuits, Batchelor's Foods, S W Berrisford, Bettacater, Brooke Bond Oxo, Cadbury Schweppes Foods, Carnation Foods, Cirio Co, Donald Cook and Son, S Daniels, Del Monte, Deltec Foods, Dewars, SFK Foods, Gilbert and John Grenall, John Harvey and Son, ICCG, Kellogg Company of Great Britain, T Lucas and Co, Libbys, Londegg, Mars, McDougall, Merrydown Wine Co, Nabisco Foods, L E Pritchett, Quaker, Ryvita Co, Shippams, Simpsons Readifood, Smedleys, Sutherlands, Unigate Foods, United Rum Merchants, Universal Foods and Whitworths.

APPENDIX 5

Medical

AMONGST MY MANY OTHER responsibilities it was inevitable that my position as team doctor would not achieve the same depth of preparations as other doctors would have put into similar expeditions.

Early on in the planning, I had sent a questionnaire around which everyone was required to fill in, enquiring about significant past medical history, including haemorrhoids, more commonly known as piles, extolling everyone to make sure that smallpox, cholera, typhoid and tetanus injections were up-to-date, and asking individuals to visit the dentist for a check-up.

Infective hepatitis is prevalent in Nepal and injections of gamma-globulin give short-lasting immunity. Gamma-globulin is hard to come by and the injections are expensive and were not insisted upon, although several of the expedition members thought it a wise precaution to be covered.

Satisfied that everyone was fit for the trip, I began looking at the problems we were likely to meet and collecting drugs accordingly. I have reproduced my list along with brief explanatory notes for the benefit of those individuals who find themselves appointed as the 'team doctor'.

1. Anti-Malarials. There is little malaria in Nepal although it is a wise precaution to take anti-malarials. Daraprim tablets only need to be taken once a week.

2. Antibiotics. For chest infections, tonsillitis, infected wounds, etc, a stock of antibiotics, eg Ampicillin, Oxetetracycline are essential.

3. Antidiarrhoeals. The most effective are Lomotil tablets and Codeine Phosphate tablets.

4. Analgesics (pain-killers). Mild: Aspirin, Distalgesic.

185

Moderate: Fortral, Codeine tablets. Severe: Morphine injections. Pain from one cause or another, eg wounds, headache, accident, is inevitable. A selection of 'pain-killers' is essential. For severe pain, eg fractures, an injectable form is advisable, eg Morphine. Piles can be very painful, Anusol suppositories and a local anaesthetic cream are required.

5. Antiseptic. Antiseptic cream, eg Savlon for putting on cuts and grazes, and solution, eg Hibitane for cleaning large wounds is essential. Medi-swabs for cleaning injection sites are useful.

6. Antihistamines. 'Anti-itch' and 'Anti-allergic' drugs. Piriton tablets are well-known to most hay fever sufferers. Antihistamine cream, many brands of which are available over the chemist counter, are extremely effective for itching, irritating bites and stings. An insect repellent cream is useful of course, in prevention.

7. Ear drops. Antibiotic-steroid ear drops are invaluable as a blind cure for earache.

Eye drops or ointment. Antibiotic eye ointment is invaluable for styes and eye infection. Steroid eye drops are required for snow blindness.

8. Hypnotics (Sleeping pills). Sleeping is difficult at altitude and under uncomfortable conditions. Mogadon tablets give a good night's sleep and have few side effects.

9. General dressing materials. A plentiful supply of these is required, eg Elastoplasts, dry dressings, Elastoplast tape, crepe bandages, cling bandages, paraffin gauze, antibiotic spray, spray-on wound dressings and plaster of paris bandages for fractures.

10. Dentistry kit. A dentist's mirror, dentist's excavator, dental spatula and emergency filler should be taken. Exposed nerve roots and missing fillings can make life a misery. It is an easy matter to mix a little paste and put in a temporary filling.

11. Suture materials. Catgut and silk with needles. Local anaesthetic, syringes and needles, needle-holder, scissors, forceps. Generally someone can be found who knows how to stitch. If not it's an easy matter to learn in a few minutes.

12. Altitude emergencies. (1) Frusemide injection for

pulmonary oedema. (2) Dexamethasone injection, which is a potent steroid for cerebral oedema.

Altitude sickness is a life-threatening emergency and of course the best line of treatment is prevention which entails careful acclimatisation. Should altitude sickness occur, then it is essential to get the patient down to low altitude, and if medical personnel are available then both Frusemide and Dexamethasone may be given. Diagnostic equipment consisted of a clinical thermometer, Littmann stethoscope, a pocket auriscope-ophthalmoscope set donated by Keeler Instruments Ltd. In addition, an emergency oxygen cylinder and face mask supplied by Philip Harris Ltd was taken.

I attempted to keep my list small and basically simple, so that in my absence for one reason or another anyone could take over the role of medical officer. As it was the entire kit fitted into a briefcase-sized bag.

Of course there were deficiencies, but I based my planning on not becoming involved with treating the local population, believing that sporadic medical attention by passing trekkers is worse than no medical treatment at all, being geared up to handle those emergencies I felt able to, and using the back-up facilities of Khunde Hospital and, if necessary, a helicopter evacuation to Kathmandu for serious emergencies.

By and large we had no major problems. On our training in Austria two small lacerations were sutured and one broken tooth temporarily repaired until a more permanent treatment could be made.

On the journey overland, we ate our own food for much of the time and were meticulous over sterilising water, and, apart from the occasional tummy upset, had no serious casualties.

Once the expedition got under way and once we left Kathmandu, we experienced problems due to the climate. In the warm and wet monsoon conditions it was inevitable that any cut, blister, or leech bite would rapidly become infected and this was to prove a major problem, in particular with one member of the expedition who was already suffering from psoriasis of the skin. A plentiful supply of antiseptic cream, dressings and Elastoplast are essential to try to give wounds and cuts the best possible chance of healing up.

Diarrhoea and dysentery is an inevitable problem in Asia. Personal hygiene and cleanliness cannot combat the lack of sewage disposal facilities and piped water, and it can only offset the attacks of gastro-enteritis. Mild antidiarrhoeal mixtures have little effect on the ravages of the 'Kathmandu Quickstep' and hefty doses of Lomotil and Codeine Phosphate were required in our own case.

Weight loss was universal amongst team members, partly due to repeated attacks of gastro-enteritis, which seriously debilitated two individuals, and also to the gradual process of becoming fitter and shedding those few extra pounds of surplus body fat.

Piles are common at altitude and aggravated by going higher, due to increased congestion in the rectal veins and to my eternal embarrassment after haranguing the rest of the team to make sure they were a hundred per cent fit, I seemed to suffer more than most from this extremely painful condition. Anusol suppositories and a plentiful supply of pile ointment are essential.

Snow blindness is not a problem frequently encountered on canoe expeditions and both Mick Reynolds and I made the elementary mistake of leaving snow glasses off in the deceptively dull conditions around Base Camp. The reflection from the snow was considerable and Mick Reynolds was mildly affected whilst my own eyes were very painful and my eyesight defective for several days.

Despite our short acclimatisation period, apart from general lethargy, headaches and listlessness, we coped well with altitude. We would, I feel, have been well advised to stop off for several days and reduce the risk of developing altitude sickness, but, desperately short of time and with the monsoon coming to a close, we felt that the dangers of shooting straight up to altitude and then back down again were acceptable.

In summary, no one should be put off by the medical problems of an expedition. A little reading, advice on building up a medical kit, and plenty of common sense would put anyone in a position to cope with the majority of medical problems we met on our own expedition.

References:
Expedition Travel and Your Health by Peter Steele (Bristol University, 1975).
Mountain Medicine by Michael Ward (Crosby Lockwood Staples, 1975).
Everest the Hard Way by Chris Bonington. Appendix on Medicine by Charles Clark (Hodder and Stoughton, 1976).

Acknowledgments:
Beechams, Philip Harris Medical, Keeler Instruments, and Eli Lily.

Glossary of Terms

Breakout: area of slack water or eddy in which it is safe to stop.

Cataract: a series of stepped rapids.

C Class boat: Canadian class canoe paddled kneeling with single bladed paddle.

C1: single Canadian class canoe with one person in it.

C2: double Canadian class canoe with two people in it, one paddling on the right, one on the left hand side.

Chang: Sherpa beer made from rice, millet or corn.

Chi (Chai): tea.

Choke or rock choke: a mass of jumbled boulders blocking the route.

Chute: a fast flowing stretch of fairly smooth water between two obstacles.

Crampons: steel spiked frames fitted to climbing boots to give a grip on ice and firm snow slopes.

Current: moving water.

Dahl: a pealike plant; a purée of pulse.

Deck: neoprene skirt worn around the waist and making a watertight seal between canoe and canoeist. Also called a sprayskirt.

Draw stroke: a technique of using the paddle held at right angles to the canoe to move the canoe sideways.

Eddy or breakout: an area of slack water behind an obstruction in the river bed.

Eskimo roll: a series of underwater paddle strokes by which the upturned canoe is righted.

Fall: a large rapid with an appreciable drop over a short distance.

Ferry glide: the technique of crossing the current by paddling the canoe at an acute angle upstream.

Grades: a system by which the severity of rapids is indicated. The following definitions of grades have been used in this book:

Grade 1: smooth moving water

Grade 2: moving water, occasional rocks

Grade 3: moving water with rocks

Grade 4: large falls but not continuous

Grade 5: long continuous unbroken stretches of rapids

Grade 6: the hardest grade there is, with ultimate risk to life

Haystack: an exploding wave with a broken foaming top which curls over on itself.

Hole: water at a lower level than that of the main river, caused by eddies behind a large obstacle, moving in the opposite direction to the flow.

Karabiners: metal snap-links used for attaching ropes to an anchor.

Kayak: canoe with built in seat, paddled sitting down.

K1: type of kayak paddled by a single canoeist, seated with a double-ended paddle.

Loop: when the canoe stands vertically in the water.

Prussiking: a method of ascending or descending a rope with the aid of prussik knots or friction hitches, with foot loops.

Rakshi: a spirit distilled from rice.

Rapid: a series of water and rock hazards.

Seal launch: a method of entering the water by sliding down a short bank either forwards or sometimes sideways, with the paddler already seated in the canoe.

Sirdar: the head Sherpa.

Standing wave: un unbroken stationary wave in a river caused by an underwater obstruction such as a boulder.

Stopper: a stationary wave which is breaking. Technically known as a hydraulic jump.

Tsampa: barley based flour.

Whirlpool: a vortex of water.